HOSPITALITY HRM

DR ANSHUMALI PANDEY

Contents

1. Introduction To Human Resource Management   1

2. Recruitment, Learning & Development, Performance 34
   Appraisal

3. Employee Motivation, Compensation And Benefit   112
   Management

4. Job Satisfaction, Organisational Culture, Disciplinary 162
   Action

The Author   213

ONE

INTRODUCTION TO HUMAN RESOURCE MANAGEMENT

Introduction:

The revolution in the Information technology has brought significant and drastic changes in our day-to-day life. Indian software professionals made significant strides in the information technology industry of USA. Employees of Rourkela Steel Plant turned the loss-making unit into a profit-making company, whereas most of the public sector companies like Hindustan Machine Tools Ltd. (HMT), and Hindustan Cables Ltd., became sick. Thus, there is several numbers of live examples available where people or employee can make or mar an organization. Therefore every company or organization is deeply interested in having an answer to this question that How to induce the employees or people to make an organization but not to mar it.

Today it is unanimously accepted by all the organizations that Human resource or manpower has a paramount importance in the success of any organization because most of the problems in organizational setting are human and social rather than physical, technical or economical failure. In the words of Oliver Shelden, —No industry can be rendered efficient so long as the basic fact remains unrecognized that it is principally human.

CONCEPT OF HRM

HRM is concerned with the human beings in an organization. —The management of man‖. Though it is a very important and challenging job because of the dynamic nature of the employees .As no two people are similar in nature – in every aspect of mental abilities, tacticians, sentiments, and behaviors; they differ widely not only individually but also as a group and are subjected to many varied influences. People are responsive, they feel, think and act therefore they cannot be handled like a machine or shifted and altered like template in a room layout. They therefore need a tactful handing by management personnel.‖

HRM is the process of managing people of an organization with a human approach. Human resources approach to manpower enables the manager to view the people as an important resource. It is the approach through which organization can utilize the manpower not only for the benefits of the organization but for the growth, development and self satisfaction of the concerned people.

Thus, HRM is a system that focuses on human resources development on one hand and effective management of people on the other hand so that people will enjoy human dignity in their employment.

Definition:

In general Human Resource Management is a management function concerned with hiring, training, motivating, developing and maintaining workforce in an organization. Human resource management ensures satisfaction of employees so as to get maximum contribution of employees for the achievement of organizational objectives.

According to **Armstrong (1997)**, Human Resource Management can be defined as —a strategic approach to acquiring, developing, managing, motivating and gaining the commitment of the organization's key resource – the people who work in and for it.‖

According to Dale Yoder —the management of human resource is viewed as a system in which participants seeks to attain both individual and group goals.‖

According to Flippo —HRM is the planning, organizing, directing and controlling of the procurement, development, compensation, integration, maintenance and reproduction of human resources to the end that individual organizational and societal objectives are accomplished ‖

Nature of HRM:

It includes:

>   1. HRM is based on certain principles and
>   policies which helps the organization to

achieve its objectives.

2. HRM is a pervasive function – It suggest that HRM is not associated to a single department, instead it is a broader function and is spread throughout the organization, which manages all type of employees/people from lower level to top level departments of the organization.

3. HRM is people oriented – The main core or concern for HRM is the People or human resource. Human resource management works with and for people. It acts as a bridge which brings people and organization together to achieve individual and organizational goals.

4. HRM is continuous activity – As HRM needs to continuously train, develop, or replace to meet the growing level of competition and changes in the market. Hence, it is a continuous activity.

5. The HRM is a part of management function. Issues like hiring, training, development, compensation; motivation, communication, and administration etc of employees are taken care by Human resource management.

6. The main aim of HRM is optimum utilization of employees.

Objectives of HRM:

The main objective of HRM is to ensure that there are right people for right jobs so that the organizational goals are achieved effectively. Beside that:-

1. To help the organization to attain its goals effectively and efficiently by providing competent and motivated

employees.

2. To utilize the available human resources effectively.
3. To increase to the fullest the employee's job satisfaction and self-actualization.
4. To develop and maintain the quality of work life (QWL) which makes employment in the organization a desirable personal and social situation.
5. To help maintain ethical policies and behavior inside and outside the organization.
6. To establish and maintain cordial relations between employees and management.
7. To reconcile individual/group goals with organizational goals.

Scope of Human Resource Management:

1. **Personnel Aspect**

Human Resource Planning – It is the process by which the organization identifies the number of jobs vacant.

- **Job Analysis and Job Design** – Job analysis is the systematic process for gathering, documenting, and analyzing data about the work required for a job. Job analysis is the procedure for identifying those duties or behavior that defines a job.

- **Recruitment and Selection** – Recruitment is the process of preparing advertisements on the basis of information collected from job analysis and publishing it in newspaper. Selection is the process of choosing the best candidate among the candidates applied for the job.

- **Orientation and Induction** – Making the selected candidate informed about the organization's background, culture, values, and work ethics.

- **Training and Development** – Training is provided to both new and existing employees to improve their performance.

- **Performance Appraisal** – Performance check is done of every employee by Human Resource Management. Promotions, transfers, incentives, and salary increments are decided on the basis of employee performance appraisal.

- **Compensation Planning and Remuneration** – It is the job of Human Resource Management to plan compensation and remunerate.

- **Motivation** – Human Resource Management tries to keep employees motivated so that employees put their maximum efforts in work.

2. **Welfare Aspect** – Human Resource Management have to follow certain health and safety regulations for the benefit of employees. It deals with working conditions, and amenities like - canteens, crèches, rest and lunch rooms, housing, transport, medical assistance, education, health and safety, recreation facilities, etc.

3. **Industrial Relation Aspect** – HRM works to maintain co-ordinal relation with the union members to avoid strikes or lockouts to ensure smooth functioning of the organization. It also covers - joint consultation,

collective bargaining, grievance and disciplinary procedures, and dispute settlement.

Functions of HRM:

We have already defined HRM and suggested that it is a management function ie it is based on what managers do and the functions performed by managers are common to all organizations. For the convenience of study, the function performed by the resource management can broadly be classified into two categories, ie Managerial functions and Operative functions

1. **Managerial Functions**: It includes Planning, Organizing, Staffing, Directing and controlling (POSDC)

   a. **Planning**: Planning is to plan for future or predetermine the course of actions to be taken in future. It is a process of identifying the organizational goals and formulation of policies and programmes for achieving those goals.

   b. **Organizing**: Organizing is a process by which the structure and allocation of jobs are determined. Thus organizing involves giving each employee a specific task establishing departments, delegating authority to subordinates, establishing channels of authority and communication, coordinating the work of subordinates, and so on.

   c. **Staffing**: This is a process by which managers select, train, promote and remove their employees This involves deciding what type of people should be hired, recruiting, selecting employees, setting the performance standard, compensation of employees, evaluation of performance of employees, counseling employees, training and developing employees.

d. **Directing/Leading**: Directing is the process of initiating or activating group efforts to achieve the desired organizational goals, which includes activities like getting subordinates to get the job done, maintaining their morale, motivating subordinates etc, for achieving the organizational goals.

e. **Controlling**: It is the process of setting the standards for performance, measuring the actual performance of the employees and then comparing the actual performance with the standards and there by taking corrective actions as needed.

1. **Operative Functions**: The Management functions as suggested were common to all the mangers where as the Operative, also called as service functions are relevant to specific department only. These functions differ from department to department depending upon the nature of the department. Viewed from this standpoint, the operative functions of HRM relate to ensuring right people for right jobs at right times. These functions include procurement, development, compensation, and maintenance functions of HRM. A brief description of these follows:

a. **Procurement:** It involves procuring the right kind of people in the right or rather appropriate number to be placed in the organization. It consists of activities such as manpower planning, recruitment, selection placement and induction or orientation of new employees.

b. **Development:** It includes activities meant to improve the knowledge, skills aptitudes and values of employees so as to enable them to perform their jobs in a better manner in future. It comprises of training to employees, executive training to develop managers, organization development to strike a better fit between organizational climate/culture and employees.

c. **Compensation:** Compensation function involves determination of wages and salaries which should match with the contribution made by employees towards achieving organizational goals. In other words, this function ensures equitable and fair remuneration for employees in the organization. It consists of activities such as job evaluation, wage and salary administration, bonus, incentives, etc.

d. **Maintenance:** It is concerned with retaining or protecting and promoting employees while at work. For this purpose several benefits such as housing, medical, educational, transport facilities, etc. is provided to the employees. Several other social security measures such as provident fund, pension, gratuity, group insurance, etc. are also being given to the employees.

Importance of HRM:

Human resources play a crucial role in the development process of modern economics. The importance of human resource management:

1. **Social Significance**: Proper management of employees/people helps in enhancing their dignity by satisfying their social needs. This is done by:

   - HRM maintains a balance between the jobs available and the jobseekers, according to the qualifications and needs.
   - HRM helps in providing healthy work environment, which might bring them psychological satisfaction
   - HRM makes the maximum utilization of the resources in an effective manner and paying the employee a reasonable compensation in proportion to the contribution made by him
   - By helping people make their own decisions, and supporting their decisions.

2. **Professional Significance**: By providing healthy working environment it promotes team work in the employees. This is done by:

   - Maintaining the dignity of the employee as a _human-being'

- Providing maximum opportunity for personal development
- Providing healthy relationship between different work groups so that work is effectively performed
- Improving the employees' working skill and capacity
- Correcting the errors of wrong postings and proper reallocation of work.

3. **Significance for Individual Enterprise:** It can help the organization in achieving its goals by:

- Generating right attitude among the employees through effective motivation
- Utilizing effectively the available goals of the enterprise and fulfilling their own social and other psychological needs of recognition, love, affection, belongingness, esteem and self-actualization.

4. **Nation's Well-being:** A nation might be rich in physical resources will not get its benefit itself, unless human resource makes proper use of them. In fact, human resources with right attitude are solely responsible for making use of national resources and for the transformation of traditional economies into the modern industrial and knowledge economies

5. **Man *vis-à-vis* Machine:** Most of the problems in organization are human and social rather

than physical, technical or economic. No industry can be considered efficient, as long as the basic fact remains unrecognized that it is principally human. It is not a mass of machines and technical processes but a body of men.

Thus not only the Dynamic and growth - oriented organizations requires an effective management of people in a fast - changing environment. Organizations flourish only through the efforts and competencies of their human resources. Employee capabilities must continuously be acquired, sharpened, and used. Any organization will have proper human resource management

- To improve the capabilities of an individual
- To develop team spirit of an individual and the department
- To obtain necessary co - operation from the employees
- To promote organizational effectiveness this in turn will help in overall development of the society as a whole and thereby causing overall growth and development of the nation.

GROWTH DRIVERS OF HRM IN INDIA:

The history of development of HR management in India is not very old rather it is of recent origin. Though if we search ancient era, there are facts available that Kautilya had dealt with some of the important aspects of Human Resources Management in his Arthasastra, written in 400 B.C. Rulers of those days adapted the techniques of HRM as suggested by Kautilya. In its modem sense, it has developed and gained popularity only since independence.

Though the importance of labor officers was recognized as early as 1929, Royal Commission Report on labor in India, which recommended the appointment of labor officers to solve labor and welfare problems, gained momentum only after the enactment of the Factories Act of 1948.

Section 49 of the Act directed the appointment of Welfare Officers in the companies having more than 500workers. In the beginning; Government was concerned only with limited aspects of labor welfare. The earliest labor legislation in India dealt with certain aspects of Indian laborers (Regulation of Recruitment, Forwarding and Employment) sent to various British colonies in 1830.

Recent Developments: Recent developments in the area of human resources management include treating the employees as economic, social, psychological and spiritual men and women. The important aspects of development of human resources management year wise is shown below:

- From the year 1995, emphasis has been shifted to human resources development (HRD).
- In the year 1998, emphasis on HRD, cultural diversity, teamwork and participative management has been continuing. Further, the emerging areas are total quality in management in HRM, empowering the employees and developing empowered teams and integrating HRM with strategic management as the top management, realized that HRM is the core of competencies of the 21st century corporations.
- In the year 1999, second National Commission on Labor was setup to study the labor conditions.

- In the year 2001, emphasis has been on 'smart sizing of the organizations'.
- In the year 2002, emphasis has been shifted to positive attitude of the candidate/employee rather than skill and knowledge.
- In the year 2003, shift from intelligence quotient (IQ) to emotional quotient (EQ).
- In the year 2004, shift from skilled workers to knowledge workers.
- In the year 2005, shift from hierarchical structure to flexible and virtual structures.
- In the year 2006, HRM has become the core of strategic management level.
- In the year 2007, the concept of HRM has been relegated to human capital management.
- In the year 2008, emphasis has been on retention management and development of own human resources by companies through alliances with universities/colleges. In the same year, there was decline in business operations due to global economic recession and crisis.
- In the year 2009, continuation of job cuts, pay costs and lay-offs due to prolonged global recession and crisis.

- In the year 2014, emphasis is shifted to talent management and flexible human resource policies and practices.

ROLE OF HRM:

Human Resources Management plays the most crucial role in the management of an organization. The role of HRM is to plan, develop and administer policies and programs designed to make optimum utilization of the organization's human resources. It is that part of management which is concerned with the people at work and their relationship within enterprises. According to R.L Mathis and J. H. Jackson (2010) several roles can be fulfilled by HR management. The nature and extent of these roles depend on both what upper management wants HR management to do and what competencies the HR staff have demonstrated. Three roles are typically identified for HR.

- Administrative
- Operational Actions
- Strategic HR

1. **Administrative Role of HR:** The administrative role of HR management is concerned with the administration and record keeping including essential legal paperwork and policy implementation. Earlier it was a tedious job but with the advancement of technology the record keeping is becoming easy and huge data can be easily stored.

2. **Operational and Employee Advocate Role for HR:** HR managers manage most HR activities in concern with the strategies and operations that have been determined by management and serves as employee —champion‖ for employee issues and concerns.HR generally has been viewed as the —employee advocate‖ in organizations. As they act as the voice for employee in front of the management specifying employees issues and concerns,

and spend considerable time on HR —crisis management,‖ dealing with employee problems that are both work-related and non work-related. Employee advocacy helps to ensure fair and equitable treatment.

The operational role requires HR professionals to co-operate with various departmental and operating managers and supervisors in order to identify and implement needed programs and policies in the organization.

3. **Strategic Role of HR:** The administrative role (of record keeping) traditionally was the major or prominent role of HR. But with the changing scenario, a broader transformation in HR is needed so that significantly less HR time and fewer HR staffs are used just for clerical work. Differences between the operational and strategic roles exist in a number of HR areas. The strategic HR role means that HR professionals are required to be more proactive in taking care of business realities and focusing on future business needs, such as strategic planning, compensation strategies, the performance of HR and measuring its results. However, in some organizations, HR often does not play a key role in formulating the strategies for the organization as a whole; instead it merely carries them out through HR activities.

Many executives, managers, and HR professionals today are increasingly seeing the need for HR management to become a greater strategic contributor towards the business success of organizations. HR should be responsible for knowing what the true cost of human capital is for an employer. Today it is expected that the HR should get involve in formulating strategies for the organization besides implementing the strategies. Today the role of HR is shifted from a facilitator to a functional peer with competencies in other functions and is acknowledged as an equal partner by others. The department has the responsibility for monitoring employee satisfaction, since it is consider as a substitute to customer satisfaction.

According to McKinsey's 7-S framework model HR plays the role of a catalyst for the organization and as per his framework, the organizational change is based on seven S's (Strategy, Structure, Systems Style, Staff, Skills and Super-ordinate Goals).Clearly, all the S's have to complement each other and are needed to be aligned towards a single corporate vision for the organization to be effective. It has been realized that most of the S's are determined directly or indirectly by the way Human Resources are managed and therefore, HRM must be a part of the total business strategy.

Role of HR Manager:

Human Resources Manager plays a vital role in the modem organization. He plays various strategic roles at different levels in the organization. Some of the common roles of the HR manager include:

The Conscience Role: The conscience role is that of a role of moral teacher or guru who reminds the management of its morals and obligations which they have towards their employees.

The Counselor : HR manager act as a counselor for the employees who are not satisfied with the present job approach, beside that employees are facing various other problems like marital, health, etc for that also the HR Manager counsels and consults the employees and offers suggestions to solve/overcome the problems.

The Mediator: As a mediator, the HR manager plays the role of a peace-maker and settles the disputes between employees and the management.

The Spokesman: HR manager act as a spokesman for or representative of the company as well as for the employees.

The Problem-solver: He also acts as a problem solver and solves the issues related to the human resources management and overall long range organizational planning.

The Change Agent: He acts as a change agent and brings changes in various existing programmes so as to keep the organization and employees update as according to the current scenario.

CHARACTERISTICS OF THE HOSPITALITY INDUSTRY:

The first thing for the HR to do while designing and drafting the business strategies and policies for any industry, is to have in-depth knowledge of its most important product. We belong to Hospitality Industry so it is essential here to understand for Human resource to understand the basic characteristics or features of Hospitality industry before laying down the policy for Hospitality Industry. Following are the characteristics of Hospitality Industry:

Intangibility: Intangible service means the things which can be felt only and cannot take along with you. Hospitality & Tourism products are mostly services and, most of them intangible in nature though with tangible, concrete elements. A basic meaning of intangibility is that the properties of hospitality products cannot be transmitted, displayed or tested in advance. It is their use, feelings, memories which is transmitted. This means that the purchased product is unique and, in contrast to tangible products, tourism products are fundamentally experiences. Besides, intangibility implies that buyers are not sure about what they buy or about what they will get.

Perishable: Hospitality products cannot be stored so, unless consumed and if not planned, they are waste. Perishable service characteristic in hospitality industry means they won't last long and will not be able to experience the same experience. For Example Airplane Seat if not booked will go empty forever revenue loss for that day.

Aggregating: A tourism product can be formed by aggregating or combining various products, and this makes its commercialization and quality control very difficult. Prices can vary by eliminating or adding services to the existing pack, creating new, customized, products.

Heterogeneity: Hospitality products are **heterogeneous in nature ie they are of mix nature as they are** formed by combining various products, and this makes its commercialization and quality control more difficult.

Simultaneous production and consumption: As most of the products are created, stored, purchased and then used, hospitality products are purchased first and then produced and consumed simultaneously, at the same place and time. This means that services cannot be separated from their guest or consumer and, therefore, consumers have to travel to the location of the product, not vice versa. For this reason, the human component in the provision of services is extremely important

HR CHALLENGES:

The most critical challenge of Human Resource department in hospitality industry is employment-related. According to the International Society of Hospitality Consultants suggest that labor and skills shortages as among the industry's top 10 challenges. As seen more people are leaving than entering the hospitality workforce, keeping hotels, restaurants and other hospitality businesses short-handed. The reasons suggested in the report are substandard wages as one of the most important reason by which hospitality industry in India is not able to retain and attract skilled workers. Beside those Long hours, including nights and weekends make jobs in the industry undesirable career choices for college- educated.

Some major challenges faced by HR in hospitality industry in India are:

- **Turnover** -As already mentioned High Turnover is a major problem for HR in the hospitality sector. According to a survey by the Bureau of Labor Statistics, leisure and hospitality had some of the highest turnover rates, with an average between 4.8 and 5.5 percent from February to June 2013. Varied schedules, Job Shifts and low pay with lot of work pressure are some of the major reasons of high turnover in hospitality industry.

- **Recruitment** -With relatively high turnover rates, Next problem that comes with no surprise is that of recruiting the right type of employee at the right time and at right position is a huge challenge for the HR in the hospitality industry. Even finding candidates with the skills to clear at entry-level positions has become an issue. When an establishment fails to fully assess real caliber of candidates, it increases the chances of placing the right person on the wrong job.

- **Training**- With high turnover next problem that comes for HR is training problems, as when the rate of retention is low, management put pressure to hire new recruits on the job before even teaching or training them how to do the job properly. Thereby putting undue pressure on new joiners and putting questions on the standards of service thereby causing undue problem on HR.

- **Morale** -Maintaining the morale of the employee has become one of the major problems faced by HR. Low morale has a large impact on service standards, which can destroy the reputation of a hotel. The causes of low morale can vary by business, but some of the major reasons for are lack of training, unskilled colleagues, understaffing, stress and few rewards.

- **Globalization** - Due to growing internationalization and globalization of business, it has its impact on HRM in terms of problems of unfamiliar laws, languages, practices, competitions, attitudes, management styles, work ethics and more.

- **New Organizational forms** - Today the basic challenge for HRM comes from the changing character of competitions. Now competition is not between individual firms but between groups of firm. Most of the companies are operating through a complex web of strategic alliances, forgings with local suppliers etc. These relationships give birth to completely new forms of complex organizational structure, and HRM has to cope with the need of these newly networked relations instead of more comfortable hierarchical relationships that existed for ages in the past within the organizations.

- **Change in Demographics of Workforce-** Nowadays changes in workforce can be easily seen for example dual career couples, working mothers, more educated and aware workers etc. These dynamic and aware workforces have their own needs from HR and from HRM perspective it is a true challenge to handle.

- **Change in employee expectations-** As mentioned earlier with the changes in workforce demographics, employee expectations and attitudes have also changed. Now the old and traditional attractions of job like job security, house, and remunerations are not much attractive today, rather today employees are demanding empowerment and equality with management. This is becoming a challenge for HRM to redesign the profile of workers, and discover new methods of hiring, training, remunerating and motivating employees.

- **Contribution to the success of organizations**: - The biggest challenge for HR manager is to bring coordination between employee and the management and make all employees work towards the success of the organization in an ethical and socially responsible way. As society's well being is also depended to a large extent on its organizations.

MAN POWER PLANNING:

Manpower Planning also called as Human Resource Planning suggest of putting right number of people, right kind of people at the right place, at right time, and doing the right things for which they are selected and suited for the achievement of goals of the organization. Human Resource Planning has got an important place in the arena of industrialization.

As according to Geisler, —Manpower planning or HR Planning is the process which includes forecasting, developing and controlling by which a organization ensures that it has-

- The right number of people,
- The right kind of people,
- At the right places,
- At the right time, doing work for which they are economically most usefull.

Manpower planning as defined by stainer is the —strategy for the requisition, utilization, improvement and preservation of an enterprise's human resource. It relates to establishing job specifications or the quantitative requirements of jobs determining the number of personnel required and developing sources of manpower. Thus Manpower planning is a process determining the requirement of right number and right kind of human force at right place and right time.

Need of Manpower Planning/HRP:

Manpower Planning is actually a two-phase process as manpower planning not only make the analyses of the current or present human resource requirement but also makes manpower forecasts for future and thereby help in drawing employment programmes. Manpower Planning is advantageous to firm in following manner:

1. Shortages and surplus of employees can be identified so that quick action can be taken wherever required.
2. Manpower Planning becomes the base for all the recruitment and selection programmes..
3. It helps to reduce the labor cost by keeping a check on excess staff in the firm thereby

controlling overstaffing.

4. It also helps to identify the available talents in a firm so that training programmes can be framed as accordingly to develop those talents.

5. It helps in growth and diversification of business. Through manpower planning, human resources can be readily available and they can be utilized in best manner.

6. It helps the organization to understand the importance of manpower management which finally helps in the stability of a concern.

Objectives of Manpower Planning:

Each organization needs manpower planning. An organizational unit is started to accomplish certain goals. Which requires human resources with necessary qualification? These are provided through effective manpower planning. Comprehensive manpower planning helps to optimize effectiveness of human resources. Thus the main objective of manpower planning is to ensure optimum use of human resources. Beside that the other objectives are:

- To determine present requirement level of human resource so as to ensure smooth functioning of the organization.
- To analyze and calculate future skills requirement,
- To provide control measures so as to ensure that necessary resources are available as and when required.

- To anticipate redundancies and avoid unnecessary dismissals and assess training and development needs.
- It is also needed for identifying surplus or shortage manpower areas and there by balancing manpower.

Thus in short manpower planning provides right size and structure of human resources which provides the basic infrastructure for smooth functioning of an organization. It minimizes the cost of employment and nullifies the effects of disruptions in developing and utilizing the human resources.

Process of HRP:

Human Resource Planning has to be a systems approach and is carried out in a set procedure. The procedure is as follows:

1. Analyzing the current manpower inventory
2. Making future manpower forecasts
3. Developing employment programmes
4. Design training programmes

Steps in Manpower Planning:

1. **Analyzing the current manpower inventory**-Before a manager makes forecast of future manpower, the current manpower status has to be analyzed. For this the following things have to be noted-

- Type of organization
- Number of departments
- Number and quantity of such departments
- Employees in these work units

2. **Making future manpower forecasts-** Once the factors affecting the future manpower forecasts are known, planning can be done for the future manpower requirements in several work units.

The Manpower forecasting techniques commonly employed by the organizations are as follows:

i. **Expert Forecasts**: This includes informal decisions, formal expert surveys and Delphi technique.
ii. **Trend Analysis**: Manpower needs can be projected through extrapolation (projecting past trends), indexation (using base year as basis), and statistical analysis (central tendency measure).
iii. **Work Load Analysis:** It is dependent upon the nature of work load in a department, in a branch or in a division.
iv. **Work Force Analysis:** Whenever production and time period has to be analyzed, due allowances have to be made for getting net manpower requirements.
v. **Other methods:** Several Mathematical models, with the aid of computers are used to forecast manpower needs, like budget and planning analysis, regression, new venture analysis.

3. **Developing employment programmes-** Once the current inventory is compared with future forecasts, the employment programmes can be framed and developed accordingly, which will include recruitment, selection

procedures and placement plans. **Design training programmes**- These will be based upon extent of diversification, expansion plans, development programmes etc. Training programmes depend upon the extent of improvement in technology and advancement to take place. It is also done to improve upon the skills, capabilities, knowledge of the workers.

Importance of Manpower Planning:

Human Resource Planning (HRP) is a needed for following reasons:

- Ensure optimum utilization of manpower and capitalize on the strength of HR. The organization can have a reservoir of talent at any point of time.
- To forecast future requirements and helps in controlling the availability of labor. Advance planning will help in getting continuous supply of people with desired skills who can handle challenging jobs easily.
- To be ready to face the technological, social, economic and political challenges
- To determine recruitment/induction levels. With the proper manpower planning it can decide what level of induction is required by the employees
- To determine training and development levels needs of the employees
- To know the cost of manpower if new project is being taken up.
- To assist in productivity bargaining.

- To assess in accommodation requirements which includes the physical facilities such as canteen, school, medical help, etc., can also be planned in advance.
- HRP is also responsible for motivating employee so as to reduce labor turn over.

MANAGING WORKER:

To achieve the organizational goals, employees need to motivated at all time and at all levels thus it becomes the duty of all managers especially of HR department to keep their all employees motivated so as to achieve organizational goals and as we know all employees are of different nature so their level of motivation is also different and it becomes the duty of the HR department to find and execute the ways to motivate and mange the employees in their organization so as to achieve organization goals. Workers can be managed in the following ways-

Job Design-HR should design the jobs in such a way that it creates both challenging and interesting task for the employee the job designing should be based on factors such as feedback, job significance, identifying tasks and skills. These elements should be taken into consideration in order to create dynamic and satisfying jobs for the workers.

Increased independence and authority- The HR should take care that while performing the task or work workers should have the liberty and judgment to choose the method of performing the job. The workers should be informed about the desired results in the advance and the decisions on how to complete the job should be left on the workers .This gives them more freedom to work upon the 'how to achieve' the desired outcomes. When a certain level of autonomy or freedom is provided it gives them liberty to work. But this freedom should be in controlled and monitored regularly as total autonomy will also leads to chaos.

Loyalty towards organization-The main role of a good human resource manager is to develop a feeling of faithfulness towards the organization among the workers. When the faithfulness of the employees as well as sense of belongingness towards the organization increases, their dedication and loyalty towards the job also increases. Thereby leading to less turnovers of employees with improved performance. The best way to develop faithfulness among workers is by trusting them to the maximum which helps to boost their confidence and helps them perform better.

Extensive training and development-The role of training and development in the organization can be easily seen by differentiating between a smoothly functioning organization and an unorganized one. The efficiency of workers can be increased if HR works on enhancing the employee's knowledge, skills and abilities instead of forcing them to do some work. A proper training session or a workshop can be organized to make employees more efficient.

Motivation-As already mentioned workers can only perform well if they are properly motivated. When challenging tasks are assigned to these employees they get motivated. These employees should be occupied in decision making and planning which creates a sense of belongingness. Motivation is the key way to accomplishment of the job

Communication channels-Communication is the key to achieve success in the organization which is connected with teamwork and coordination. There should not be any communication barriers among the employees. The tasks in the organization are multifaceted and require knowledge for completion which almost makes it impossible for a single person to understand or to be able to achieve everything single handed. The goals of the organization can only be achieved through teamwork.

Monitoring and evaluation-It is the responsibility of HR to regularly and systematically monitor and evaluate the performance of the employee so as to keep a control in the organization as well as to plan for desired action like training or promotion to be taken.

Work life balance-As already mentioned there is diversity in workforce nowadays so it becomes the duty of HR to ensure that employees are able to maintain a balance between work and life like employees are now days given incentive in the form of holiday package against employee excellent work where he can go the vacations with the family and can spend time with family thereby maintaining a balance between work and life.

SUMMARY:

It has been a proved fact that if business want to be successful in the market, it need to keep a balance or control on 4 M's of business ie Men , Material, Money & Machine and as already discussed if human or men resources are neglected or not managed well organization will not be able to do well. Human Resource Management is concerned with the people or employee dimension of management in the organization. HRM is the function performed in organizations that helps in most effective use of employees in the organization to achieve the organization and individual goals.

The passage of time has seen huge development in the working of HRM from administrative role to now the strategic role. HRM has gain huge importance in almost all the industries including hospitality industry.

The biggest challenge of HR managers today is to recognize talent and nurture them carefully to achieve organization and individual goals

To find out the right man for the right job and develop him into an effective team member is itself a challenging job for any manager. To fully utilize the human resources so as to achieve organizational goal, it is essential to have a proper manpower plan, as HR planning is a forward looking function which as per its process tries to assess manpower requirements in advance keeping in view production schedules, market fluctuations, demand forecasts etc in the background. The focus of the plan is to get the right number of employees at the right time and in right number.

HRM also tries to manage his employees or talent reservoir by adopting different methods and offering different challenges to judge the potentials of employees and to keep them ready to meet the current competitions.

KEY TERMS:

- **Employee development**: Employee development is the specific education and training of new employees. Employee development can also refer to an employee's continued education or retraining.

- **Employment law**: it is a set of laws that affect workplace conduct and fair practices.
- **HRM**: A process of aligning people and organization so that the goals of each are achieved effectively and efficiently.
- **HRP**: Process of identifying human resource needs and formulating plans to meet these needs.
- **Management**: the process by which objectives of organizations are achieved by the organization with and through people.
- **Management Process**: Planning, organizing followed by staffing, leading and controlling are five basic function of management.
- **Performance review**: A performance review is a written evaluation of an employee's success to show how well he or she has performed for a specific amount of time.
- **Retention**: It is the process of keeping skilled, successful employees at a specific company.
- **Trend Analysis**: Study of a firm's past employment needs over a period of years to predict future needs.
- **Work Ethic:** Work should give satisfaction to the people. If the person is satisfied with the work, he can perform more, it reflects in the growth of the organization as well as individuals.
- **Work Life Balance**: Work-life balance is achieved when an individual's right to a fulfilled life inside and outside paid work is accepted and respected as the norm, to the mutual benefit of the individual, business and society.

TWO

RECRUITMENT, LEARNING & DEVELOPMENT, PERFORMANCE APPRAISAL

INTRODUCTION:

As already proved that the human resources are the most important assets for the organization. The failure or success of any organization is highly based on the competence of the manpower working in that organization.

Thus in order to achieve the organization objectives, the organization especially HR needs to recruit manpower with requisite skills, qualifications and experience. While doing so the HR needs to take into consideration both present and future requirements of the organization in the mind.

After the employees have been selected for various positions in the organization, training them the assigned task becomes the priority of the organization so as to avoid future problems. Training act as breaking period where a new employee gets a chance to adjust to the new environment. Training involves enhancement in the knowledge, skills and abilities of the employee so that they can fit for meeting the requirements of the organization. Whereas learning is an ongoing process where we learn the things which we were not aware of – basic to the conceptual skills making them fit for the organization. Apart from training the technical skills the executives or managerial level employees are also required to learn the techniques of dealing with people, problem solving, decision making and other conceptual skills so developing the manager and executives becomes need of the organization to prepare them for future

Every organization wants that their goals set by the organization are achieved for that employees need to put their best efforts and help the organization to achieve these predetermine goals, but every employee in the organization has a different attitude to do his job or handle the work, as some like work pressure while some avoids it thus to evaluate or identify whether an employee is putting forward his best effort or not towards the job, performance appraisal is used, to evaluate the performance of the employee. This helps the management to review the performance of each and every employee and finally take the decision, ie whether employee should be given further training or he is fit for promotion or still requires some more experience etc.

RECRUITMENT - INTRODUCTION:

Without positive, innovative and progressive contribution from the manpower, organizations cannot progress and prosper so it becomes the major responsibility of the HR Department to get the right candidate for the right job and at the right time and that too in optimum number neither less nor more so that work of the organization moves on smoothly as well as organization objectives are also achieved with no extra burden on the organization. For this HR Department is required to recruit and select right employee.

Recruitment in simple terms can be defined as Finding and Attracting Applications.

Definition: The Recruitment is the process of identifying and analyzing the job requirements, and then finding the prospective candidates, who are then encouraged and stimulated to apply for the job in the organization.

According to Edwin B. Flippo —It is the process of searching for prospective employees and stimulating and encouraging them to apply for jobs in an organization.

As per other definition —Recruitment is the process of finding and attracting capable applicants for employment‖. Where the process begins when new recruits are sought and ends when their applications are submitted. This result in a pool of applications form that new employees are selected.‖

Concept of Recruitment:

The recruitment, as defined is understood as the process of searching for and obtaining applicants for jobs, from among them the right person can be selected. Though theoretically recruitment process should said to be end with the receipt of applications, but in practice the activity further extends to the screening of applications so as to eliminate those who are not qualified for the job.

Thus Recruitment acts as a linking Function' – joining together those where jobs are to be fill and those who are seeking jobs. It act as a joining process where it tries to bring together job seekers and the employer fulfilling the needs of both, former wanting the job and later wants their jobs or position to be filled i.e. requiring manpower.

Often Recruitment and Selection are interchangeably used and confused but there is a marked difference between the two words, as recruitment itself is a positive term because it only stimulates people to apply for the job to increase the hiring ratio i.e. more number of applicants apply for the job. While selection is the negative term because it involves elimination during its process rejecting a number of candidates, leaving only those who are appropriate to be hired. Beside that Recruitment is always followed by selection so people often use the term recruitment as a whole.

Purpose and Importance of Recruitment: The importance of recruitment in the organization is as:

1. It helps to determine the present and future requirements of the organization in concurrence with personnel planning and job analysis activities

2. It increases the pool of job candidates i.e. giving more options to the organization to select from the pool the right candidate for the organization.
3. It hereby increases the success rate of selection process by reducing number of under-qualified or over-qualified applications.
4. It helps to reduce the prospect of the job applicants once selected would leave shortly
5. It helps to meet legal and social obligations
6. It helps to identify and prepare potential job applicants
7. Evaluate the effectiveness of different recruitment techniques and sources for job applicants.

Sources of Recruitment:

The sources of recruitment are broadly divided into two categories: **internal** sources and **external** sources. Both the methods have their own merits and demerits.

INTERNAL SOURCES OF RECRUITMENT: Internal sources of recruitment refer to hiring manpower from within the organization i.e. internally. This means, applicants applying for the different positions are those who are already working within the same organization.

This is an important source of recruitment, as it provides the opportunities for the development and utilization of the existing resources within the organization as performance of employees, selected is already known to the organization. Let us discuss different methods of the internal sources. It includes:

Present Employees
It includes

- **Promotions:** Promotion involves upward movement, ie upgrading the employees by evaluating their performance in the organization. It involves shifting an employee from a lower position to a higher position with more responsibilities, salary, facilities, and status. Generally many organizations fill their higher vacant positions with the process of promotions, internally.

- **Transfers:** Transfer involves lateral movement, ie process of interchanging from one job to another without any change in the rank and responsibilities. It generally involves the shifting of employees from one department to another department or one location to another location, depending upon the requirement of the organization.

- To understand how it works; let's take an example: Assume that there is a Software company called XYZ Ltd. Having two branches, Branch-A and Branch-B, but an employee from Branch-A leave his job due to some reason. Now, this position has to be filled thus, in this situation instead of searching and hiring a new candidate from outside which is time consuming and costly too, there is another possibility of shifting an employee from Branch-B to Branch-A, depending upon the requirements of the job and the capabilities of the employee. This internal shifting of an employee from one branch to another branch is called as Transfer.

- **Job Posting (Internal Advertisements):** Job posting/ Internal Advertisements is a process of posting/ advertising jobs only within the organization for example in chain groups etc. This job posting act as is an open invitation to all the employees working within /inside the organization, they can only apply for the vacant positions. It provides equal opportunities to all the employees working in the organization. Thus, the recruitment will be done from within the organization and it is cost saving too.

Past Employees

- **Recruiting Former Employees:** Recruiting former employees is another method of internal sources of recruitment, in this the ex employees who are either retired or have resigned from the organization due to some reasons are called back for rejoining as per the requirement of the job and performance of the past employee. The benefit of this method is that it is cost effective, time saving and most important is that the employee is well equipped with the roles and responsibilities of the job so the organization is not required to spend time and money on their training and development.

Employee Referrals

This concept is much popularized by BPO's or call center now followed in every field. Employee referral is an effective method of recruiting the right candidates at a low cost. In this method new candidates are hired through the references of employees, who are currently working within the same organization. In this process, the present employees are encouraged to refer their friends and relatives for filling up the vacant positions. Most of the organizations, in order to motivate their employees, to suggest referrals even provide with a referral bonus etc for a successful hire.

Previous Applicants

In this method the Hiring team plays the major role they as per the requirement of the organization checks the profiles of previous applicants from the organizational recruitment database. These applicants are basically those who have applied for jobs earlier in the past but could not get selected due to one or other reason, their CV's are kept with HR department in the form of database These resources are than approached and if organization gets a positive response they are selected for the jobs. It is also another inexpensive way of filling up the vacant positions.

Merits & Demerits of Internal Sources of Recruitment: An internal source of recruitment, i.e., hiring employees within the organization, has its own set of advantages and disadvantages.

The **advantages** are as follows:

- It is simple, easy, quick, time saving and cost effective method of recruitment.
- There is no need of induction and training, as the candidates are already aware of their job and responsibilities.
- It motivates the employees to work hard, and increases the work relationship within the organization.
- It helps in developing loyalty of the employee towards the organization.

The **disadvantages** are as follows:

- It stops the new innovative ideas and thinking to come into the organization which a new blood otherwise would have brought with him, as employee who are already working will have their own old ways of working.

- It has limited scope because all the vacant positions cannot be filled through this method.

  - There are more chances of biasness or partiality while recruiting.
  - It sometimes develops Jealousy as there could be issues in between the employees, who are promoted and who are not.
  - It may become the cause of disturbing the harmony of the organization.
  - If an internal resource is promoted or transferred, then that position will remain vacant.
  - Employees, who are not promoted, may end up being unhappy, rejected, and de- motivated.

EXTERNAL SOURCES OF RECRUITMENT:

External sources of recruitment refer to hiring employees from outside the organization externally. It suggests that, here the applicants seeking for the job are those who are external to the organization. Let us discuss different methods of the external sources:

- **Direct Recruitment:** In this method a notice of vacancy is placed on the notice board of the organization and the suitable candidates can approach the concerned person, this method of sourcing is also called as **factory gate recruitment**, as the blue-collar and technical workers are hired through this process.

- **Employment Exchanges:** Employment exchange is a government entity, where the details of the candidates requiring jobs are stored and are given to the employers for filling the vacant positions, As per the law, for certain job vacancies, it is mandatory that the organization provides details to the employment exchange. This external recruitment method is helpful in hiring employees at all levels.

- **Employment Agencies/ Professional Associations/ Consultants:** Employment agencies **/ Professional Associations/Consultants are** other good source of external recruitment. Employment agencies can be private, public, or government owned. They act as a link between the prospective candidates and employer. As they hold a database of qualified candidates and provide it to the organization as and when required by them at some cost who then select from among it. They provides unskilled, semi-skilled and skilled resources as per the requirements of the organization.

- **Advertisements:** Advertisements are the most popular and very much preferred source of external source of recruitment as they can reach to huge masses within same time and its proven fact that response through advertisement is most of the time positive. In this the job vacancy is announced through various print and electronic media – newspaper, radio etc with all the details like specific job description and specifications of the requirements. Going through the advertisement the prospective candidates can approach the organization. Thus advertisements is the best way to source mass of candidates in a short span of time and it even offers an efficient way of screening the candidates' through specific requirements mentioned in the advertisement. Though Advertisement is one of the costliest method of recruitment, but when time and number are important, then advertisement is the best source of recruitment.

- **Walk ins:** This is the most common and least expensive method for candidates as in this the job seekers submit unsolicited applications or letters or resume or bio- data to the organization and directly come for the selection process as its similar to open for all and even preferred by employers as they get a wider choice for selection for the post and moreover it is free from hassles associated with other methods of recruitment

- **Campus Recruitment:** This is another most popular source of external recruitment, where the educational institution such as colleges and universities offers opportunities to the organization for hiring their students. In this process, the organizations visit technical, management, and professional institutions for recruiting students directly for the new positions.

- **Word of Mouth Advertising:** Word of mouth is purely an intangible way of sourcing the candidates for filling up the vacant positions. As there are many reputed organizations with such high and good image in the market. That these organization names are more than enough for the job seekers. Such organizations only need a word-of-mouth advertising regarding a job vacancy to attract a large number of candidates.

· **Labor Contractors**: Manual workers or Daily wage labors can be recruited through contractors who maintain close association with the sources of such workers. This source is used to recruit labor for construction jobs.

· **Job Fairs:** Job fairs are conducted by different companies to attract candidates for entry level jobs. In this all the organization having vacancy collects at one place and organize a fair for the job seekers who can directly go to the desired counter of organization and can apply for the respective post and company, it is another good method of external recruitment as through this company can get wider choices as well as good for job seeker as get all the big brands /non brands at one place so they can choose among it and beside that its less costly than advertisements.

· **Outsourcing**: Outsourcing method involves hiring the candidates from different organization for the work and in return the organization has to pay for their services. It is similar to contractual service as for example: In India, the HR processes are being outsourced from more than a decade now. Outsourced HR Firm help the organization to create and screen the candidates for the organization for the final and further selection by the candidates for which HR firm will be paid for the services.

· **Poaching/Raiding:** This is the latest method of external recruitment being followed by the organizations today.

Poaching means hiring a competent and experienced person already working in another reputed company in the same or different industry; the organization might be a competitor in the industry. For this a company can attract talent from another company by offering attractive pay packages and other terms and conditions, better than the current employer of the candidate. Though it is seen as an unethical practice and not openly talked about but most of the Indian software and the retail sectors are facing the most severe problems due to poaching today, as it reduces the competitive strength of the firm.

- **E-Recruitment:** E-Recruitment or recruitment through internet is the use of technology to assist the recruitment process. It is gaining popularity from past few years. In this they advertise job vacancies through worldwide web. The job seekers send their applications or curriculum vitae (CV) through an e-mail using the Internet.

<u>Merits & Demerits of External Sources of Recruitment:</u>
External sources of recruitment, i.e., hiring employees from outside the organization, have both its benefits and drawbacks.
The **advantages** are as follows:

- It encourages new opportunities for the job seekers.
- It helps in increasing the branding of the organization
- There are less chances of biasness or partiality between the employees.

- There is wide scope for selecting the right candidate, because of the large number of candidates appearing.
- It brings in new ideas and innovative thinking with new blood coming in the organization.

The **disadvantages** of recruiting through external sources are as follows:

- This process is time consuming, as the selection process is very lengthy.
- Highly Expansive as compared to recruiting through internal sources.
- External candidates sometimes even demand more remuneration and benefits.
- De-motivating for the existing employees leading to poor productivity and high labor turnover
- Less Loyalty of employees towards the organization.
- Requires training
- Requires more time to adjust with the environment of the organization

Finally, the HR department should be flexible and should decide which source to select either internal or external according to the needs and requirement of the organization

What to look for in Prospective Candidates:

The ultimate aim of the recruitment and selections process is to get the right number and quality of employee's required to meet the needs of the position and ultimately to meet the needs of the organization. But it is difficult and time consuming task to get the right people into the organization. Mistakes in selecting the right candidates can have very serious consequences for the effectiveness of the organization. Three basic questions are vital for a successful recruitment which an HR should review is:

- Is the candidate competent enough for the job?
- Is the candidate motivated for the job?
- How will the candidate fit into the organization?

In order to provide answers to these questions, HR needs to be very careful in deciding the process of the recruitment and selection; it needs to be regularly and systematically analyzed, reviewed and evaluated keeping in mind the current scenario and requirement of the organization.

The four stages of recruitment and selection are:

Defining requirements: First and foremost organization needs to be very clear with the job descriptions and specification, should be prepared with the terms and conditions of employment. *Attracting candidates*: Next step is to identify, review and evaluate different sources of recruitment and then choose the best possible source of recruitment either internal or external depending upon the requirement, number and need of the organization.

Selecting candidates: Once the candidates are attracted and stimulated to apply for the job the next step is to screen and select the employees for the job which involves steps like: sifting applications, interviewing, testing, assessing candidates, employment, taking references, employment contract etc.

Introduction- induction: The final stage involves introduction of the selected candidate to the work and the colleagues, to the organization and its main objectives, and terms of employment.

Screening / Short listing: After completing the process of sourcing the candidates next step is to screening the candidates to pick the few from the pool of candidates which will further go for selection Thus screening is the process of filtering the applications of the candidates for further selection process. Screening though negative but is an integral part of recruitment process after which follows the process of selection. The screening process of recruitment consists of three steps:

Reviewing of Resumes and Cover Letters: Reviewing is the first step for screening candidates. In this step, the resumes of the candidates are reviewed and checked for the candidates' education, work experience, and overall background matching with the requirement of the job ie with

- job description
- job specification
- job terms and condition

Beside that the HR should also check for

- Reason for change of job
- Longevity with each organization

- Long gaps in employment
- Job-hopping
- Lack of career progression etc.

All these elements are checked of prospective candidates with the help of their resumes or CV and those fulfill the criteria or match with the requirements of the organization are further called for the selection process.

Selection Process: Followed by this is the selection process which involves, interviewing, employment test, assessing candidates, employment, verifying references, other verifications if required, employment contract etc , all these stages are elimination stages candidates number get reduced and only few as per requirement are finally selected.

Recruitment Policy:

The first step in planning for recruitment of employees into the organization is to establish proper policies and procedures. A policy is the standing plan, policies are directives, which assists in decision making. A recruitment policy indicates the organization code of conduct in this area of activity.

The essentials of good recruitment policy are:

- A recruitment policy should meet or in conformity with organizational objectives. it must take into consideration the basic parameters for recruitment decision.
- It should be definite, positive and clear, so that everyone in the organization should understand it.

- It should be flexible so as to meet the changing needs of an organization but at the same time it should have a high degree of permanency
- It should be formulated in such a manner that it takes care of all reasonable anticipated conditions.
- It should be based on facts and sound judgment.
- It should conform to organization economic principles, statues and regulations
- A good recruitment policy should be so designed so as to ensure career growth for its employee long term basis is it should help in developing the potentials of employees

Thus a well designed and preplanned recruitment policy based on organizational goal and needs will help the organization to appoint right type of employee for the organization.

LEARNING AND DEVELOPMENT - INTRODUCTION:

Learning and development are the process of acquiring and developing knowledge, skills, attitudes (KSA), capabilities, behaviors through learning or developmental experiences. It is concerned with ensuring that the organization has the knowledgeable, skilled, engaged and committed workforce it requires for the achievement of the objectives.

Learning – Meaning & Concept:

Learning means by which people attains and develop new knowledge, skills, capabilities, behaviors and attitudes. As defined by Honey and Mumford (1996): 'Learning happens when people display changes in KSA which they did not know before, or which cannot do before but after learning they now have acquired it (insights, realizations as well as facts) or they can do it (skills).'

According to Stephen Robbins, learning may be defined 'as any relative permanent change in behavior that occurs as a result of experience.'

These definitions of learning gives the main components of learning

- **Learning involves change**: Change may be good or bad from an organizational point of view.
- **The change should be relatively permanent**: Temporary changes may be only reflexive and fail to represent any learning.
- **Learning involves change in behavior**: Learning takes place when there is a change in actions.

Learning therefore involves changes in a behavior as a result of experience. These changes can be physical and overt, or it may involve complex intellectual or attitudinal changes which affect behavior in more subtle ways.

Thus in short Learning is a continuous process that not only enhances existing capabilities but also leads to the development of the skills, knowledge and attitudes that prepare people for enlarged or higher-level responsibilities in the future.

Development - Meaning and Concept:

Development is rich extension of training generally provided to management staff, ie it is related to enhancing the conceptual skills of the employee, which helps individual towards achieving maturity and self actualization. Development as defined as a systematic process of growth and development by which managers develop their abilities to manage. It improves the performance of the managers by providing them the opportunities for growth and development

As defined by Alan Mumford – Development involves an attempt to improve managerial effectiveness through a planned and deliberate learning process. As defined by Bernard and group -Development involves the nature and change induced among employees through process of education and training. Development cultivates those skills among the employee, application of which will improve the efficiency and effectiveness and desired outcomes of the achieving the organizational objectives are achieved.

Development is basically concerned with ensuring that a employee's ability and potential are grown which is realized through the provision of learning experiences or through self- directed (self-managed) learning. It is a process of progressing, which enables employee to progress from a present state of understanding and capability to a future state in which higher-level skills, knowledge and competencies are required.

In the field of human resource management, training and development is the field which is concerned with organizational activity aiming to improve the performance of individuals and groups in organizational settings. Thus development is also often referred to as another tool of human resource development (HRD) as it is also concerned with improving the performance of the organization as a whole and as well as of the employee with the provision of learning, development and training opportunities in order to improve individual, team and organizational performance.

Training - Meaning and Concept:

The need of training in the organization arises when it is observed that there is gap between desired or expected performance and actual performance of the employee so training is the solution used by the organization to fill or reduce the gap.

Training need = desired performance - actual performance

Training involves the use of systematic and formal processes to impart knowledge and help workers to acquire the skills necessary for them to perform their jobs satisfactorily.

It involves developing the employees so as to make them capable and confident in their jobs, and consequently in their life. Thus training is an organized process for increasing the knowledge skill and abilities (KSA) of the employees. Training is considered to be a process with an aim of changing the behavior of employee in such a way that it would result in not only in the up-liftment of the organization but also of an individual.

According to Flippo, Training is the act of increasing the knowledge and skills of an employee for doing the job in a better way. Learning is the major outcome of training. As defined by Wayne F Cascio, Training consists of planned programme with an aim to improve performance at the individual, group, and /or organizational levels. Improved performance, will in turn, reflects that there have been measurable changes in knowledge, skills attitude, and/or social behavior.

Basically training is a learning experience which is planned and carried out by the organizations to get more skilled and knowledgeable employee who are able to improve the productivity as well as are acquaint/updated with current market trends. Thus Training is considered to be one of the effective tools of Human Resource Department (HRD). As training has immense potential in transfer and utilization of latest technical know-how, leadership development, organization of people, formation of self-help-groups, mobilization of people as well as resources, empowerment of resource-poor rural mass, entrepreneurship development, etc., which are considered to be the main components of HRD.

Thus training can be understood as a process of learning a sequence of programmed behavior. It involves application of knowledge so as to improve the performance of employee on the present job and prepares them for the future job. Training is about developing people as an individual and helping them to become more confident and competent in their lives and in their jobs. The learning process is at the core of training and the ways of and opportunities for learning are numerous and varied

<u>Features of Training:</u>

- Increases knowledge and skills for doing a job
- Fill the gap between job needs and employee skills, knowledge and behaviour
- Job oriented process

Comparison between learning and training and development:

Learning can be clearly distinguished from training. 'As Learning is the process by which a person assembles new knowledge, skills and capabilities, whereas training involves one of several responses an organization generally undertake to promote learning' (Reynolds _et al_, 2002).To encourage learning use of a process model, this is concerned with facilitating the learning activities of individuals and providing learning resources for them to use. While, on other hand the provision of training use the content model, which means deciding in advance the knowledge and skills that need to be increased by training, planning the programme, deciding on training methods and presenting the content in a logical sequence through various forms of instruction. Learning is a long term program or ongoing process individual keeps on learning through his life while training is for short duration. While training is a smaller term within learning, where as learning is a bigger term.

Another distinction made by Sloman (2003) between learning and training, is learning 'lies within the domain of the individual' and training, 'lies within the domain of the organization'.

Comparison between Training & Development: Though the terms training and development appear similar or synonymous, but as suggested by Yoder, there is significant difference between these two concepts as shown in Table 2.3. As training is referred to as teaching specific skills and behavior to the employee, it is mainly associated with non managerial employee or operative staff of the organization while development involves managerial employee or manager. Beside that training is one shot deal while development is a continuous and ongoing process. Training tries to meet the current requirement of the job, employee or organization where as development aims to meet future needs employee or organization.

Learning Objectives & Process:

A learning objective is defined as a statement that describes the behavior the trainer expects participants to demonstrate as a result of the training, and can be used to evaluate the success of the session.

- To make employee as per organizational needs
- To create a climate for motivation
- Enable you to plan and gain greater control over your future
- Add challenge to your life and a sense of achievement
- Provide a means of self evaluation
- Make you results oriented, so you work smarter
- Add a new dimension of meaning to your life
- Enable you to manage your time more effectively
- Reduce the stress related to the feeling of —not getting anywhere‖
- Increase your chances of success
- Allow you to determine if your job is compatible with what you really want.

Characteristics of Learning:

1. Learning involves a purpose. Most people have a clear and definite idea of what they want to do and achieve in life.
2. Learning comes through experience. Learning is considered to be an individual process and must be done by the participant himself and the instructor cannot do this for him.
3. Learning is multifaceted.
4. Learning is an active process. The more actively a participant is involved in the class, the greater are his chances are for both learning and remembering.

THE LEARNING PROCESS:

Learning may be explained by a combination of two basic approaches: behaviorism and the cognitive theories:

- **Behaviorism Theory:** This theory believes that all living organism either humans or animals learns in about the same way. Believers of this theory stress upon the importance of having a particular form of behavior supported by someone. In this, the instructor provides the reinforcement and frequent, positive reinforcement and rewards helps in accelerating the speed of learning. It suggest, the instructor should be provided with ways to manipulate students with stimuli, to induce the desired behavior or response, and which is strengthen with appropriate rewards. In general, the behaviorist theory emphasizes positive reinforcement rather than no reinforcement or punishment.

- **Cognitive Theory:** Unlike behaviorism, the cognitive theory highlights on what is going on inside the student's mind. Cognitive supporters believe that learning is not only just a change in behavior; but it involves change in the way a learner thinks, understands, or feels. There are several branches of cognitive theory. Two of the major theories may broadly be classified as the information processing model and the social interaction model. The information processing model suggests that the student's brain has some internal structures which are responsible for selecting and processing incoming material send to them, further it is stored, retrieve it and use it to produce behavior, and receive and process feedback on the results. This involves several cognitive processes, like including executive functions of recognizing expectancies, planning and monitoring performance, encoding and producing internal and external responses.

Around 1980s.another theory named social interaction theories gained recognition. They suggested that learning and subsequent changes in behavior take place because of the interaction between the student and the environment. Behavior is modeled either by people or symbolically. Cultural influences, peer pressure, group dynamics, and film and television are some of the significant factors which influence behavior of the learner.

Thus, the social environment to which the student is exposed to or interacts with, had a huge influence on them which they reveals by demonstrating or modeling the similar behaviors, The cognitive processes include attention, retention, motor responses, and motivation.

Techniques for learning include direct modeling and verbal instruction. Behavior, personal factors, and environmental events all work together to produce learning.

- **Combined Approach:** Both the behaviorist and the cognitive approaches have their own use in terms of learning theories. A reasonable way to plan, manage, and conduct training is to include the best features of each major theory. This provides a way to measure behavioral outcomes and promote cognitive learning.

Laws of Learning: The five laws of learning are suitable for most learning situations. Keeping these laws in mind when planning a session lets the trainer creates a better learning atmosphere for the participants.

Law of Readiness: It is said that a person learns best when there is an environment for learning; he has the necessary background, a good attitude, and is ready to learn. He does not learn much if he sees no reason for learning.

Law of Exercise: As said practice makes the person perfect, so those things which are most often repeated are the best learned. This is the basis for practice and drill.

Law of Primacy: As said first impression has great impact on the receiver so trainer keeping this in mind should create first impression powerful to hold the students. This helps to provide a stable foundation for all that follows.

Law of Intensity: This law suggests that a student will learn more from the real like experiences and experiments than a substitute or classroom studies. Mockups, videotapes, interactive courseware, slides, charts, and any number of other training aids add sharpness and action to classroom instruction.

Law of Recency: As said, the things which are learned last will be best remembered for longer time. The trainer should remember law of recency when planning a good summary.

He should repeat, restate, or reemphasize the training objectives. He should also repeat important information the participants need to remember so that one lasting impression or mark is made in his mind.

Need of Training:

The main objective of training is to build the right ability and capability in the employee so that they can perform as per the requirement of the organization and helps to achieve organizational objectives.

The need for training arises to bridge the gap between actual performance and standard performance which is expected from the employee by the organization to achieve organizational objectives.

Training and development need= standard performance-actual performance The need for Training may generally due to the following reasons-

- Installation of new equipments or techniques
- Improve the efficiency of employees
- Changes in working methods or products produced
- Reduce wastage of time and money
- To get quality output
- To Reduce Accidents
- Reduce supervision
- To have preventive maintenance

- To get optimum performance
- To boost morale of employees
- To prepare workforce for future challenging work
- To plan for Promotion or transfer of employees
- To reduce absenteeism
- To bring down the grievances,
- To build career by personal growth
- To reduce wastage & breakage
- To plan for future growth

Importance of Training:

Training is importance for both the organization and the employee, on one side it helps organization to increase productivity and achieve objectives of organization while on other side it is important for the employee for his personal growth:

Benefit of Training to Organization:

- Becomes more effective in decision-making and problem-solving.
- Improve the morale of the workforce.
- Helps to make employee identify with the organizational goal.
- It helps in developing leadership skills, motivation, loyalty and better attitude among the employee.
- Improve productivity and quality of work.
- Aids in understanding and carrying out organizational policies.
- Helps in overall development of the organization.

- Creates an adequate environment for growth and communication.
- Provide opportunity to employees to adjust to the change.
- Promotes harmony in the organization
- Increase cooperation and coordination among employee
- Reduces the accidents and waste in the organization
- Helps increasing productivity and/ or quality of work
- Provides information for future needs in all areas of the organization

Benefit of Training to Employees:

- Enhancement in knowledge, skills and abilities after training.
- Helps in Increasing job satisfaction and recognition among employees.
- Helps employee to Move further step towards attaining personal goals and growth while improving interactive skills.
- Reduces the fear of attempting new tasks.
- Provides the trainee new avenue's for growth.
- Improve the morale of the trainee
- Motivational variables of recognition, achievement, growth, responsibility and advancement are some of the benefit of the training for the employee.
- Provides information for improving leadership, communication skills and attitudes.
- Helps to handle stress, tension, frustration and conflict.
- Reduces accidents and wastage.

- Helps in organizational and individual development
- Optimum Development of Human Resource

Benefits to Training to Personnel and Human Relations:

- Helps to improve inter-personnel skills.
- Helps to improves morale.
- Helps to builds cohesiveness in groups.
- Makes the organization a better place to work and live.
- Provides information on other governmental laws and administrative policies.
- Improves the job knowledge and skills at all levels of the organization.
- Helps create a better corporate image.
- Fosters authenticity, openness and trust
- Improves Organizational Culture and climate

Training Cycle:

The Training is a framework for how to plan, implement, evaluate and review the entire training process organized for the employees in the organization.

It involves following steps:

1. **Identify Training Needs:** Knowledge, skills and attitudes are the three main criteria over which all job are based. A training need is a gap between the knowledge, skills and attitudes required and those which are already possessed by the employees. An

individual training needs arise when his performance go down of standards, i.e. when there is performance deficiency. Decline in performance may be due to lack of skill or knowledge or any other problem so it becomes the responsibility of the organization to plan and organize the training programs for the employee.

Organization before starting the training process should be clear with its vision and the goals which organization wants to achieve, than they need to assess the training need of the employees of their organization, which can be based on three major human resource areas they are: the organization as a whole, the job characteristics and the needs of the individuals. This analysis will help to determine the answer to the following questions:

- Where is training needed?
- What specifically must an employee learn in order to be more productive?
- Who needs to be trained?

This can be done by identifying the current status of the organization; what is the caliber of the present employees, how work is done, what is the procedure, what they can do best etc This analysis will provide some standards and guide them to plan the training program, accordingly keeping in mind the objectives of the organization.

2. **Set Training Objectives:** Next step is to lay the training objectives, keeping in mind the above step, i.e. need of the organization; HR should set the objectives of the training. The objectives should clearly define what behavior or skill will be changed as a result of the

training and should relate to the mission and strategic plan of the firm. Objectives also help in evaluating the training program's effectiveness. Objectives of training program should always be tangible and measureable.

The objectives of training provide the following:

- A record of conditions that existed before the training was given.
- A basis for evaluation of training.

3. **Plan/Design a Training Program:** Next step involves plan or design the training program, which includes the strategy and planning through which training program will be conducted effectively. To design the training program organization should clearly state:

- Statement of objectives
- Choice of participants
- The place of training
- Duration of training program
- Pace of the training program
- The level of instruction
- Choice of training technique
- The need of feedback

4. **Implementation of Training Program:** To successfully conduct the training program, it required great efforts and coordination. Implementation involves a series of activities, like selection of trainer, i.e. the expert who will give the training; what method will be employed to give the training i.e. on the job method or off the job or the combination of both as per the requirement

and planned in the above steps; who will be the trainee, trainees should be of homogenous group with respect to experience, knowledge, and potential for learning so as to avoid gap in the group. Finally the training duration and location for training keeping in mind availability of time and budget.

5. **Evaluation of Training Program:** As the huge money and resources are spent on training, so it becomes very much important for the organization to judge or evaluate that how far the training program has been useful or successful. It not only helps to judge the effectiveness of training program but also helps to determine effectiveness of training program in terms of achievement of objective of the organization.

   Evaluation can be done on the basis of the changes occurred at three levels i.e. before the training, during the training, and after the completion of training.

6. **Review & Analysis of the Training Program:** This is the last step of training process or cycle, after evaluation of training program, the organization is able to answer following questions like:

   - Effectiveness of the training program.
   - Changes in the employee and productivity i.e. organization after training?
   - How far training program is able to achieve organizational objectives?

   Finally the organization will review and analyze the training program and decide and design for future training programs.

Training Methods:

There are two broad types of training available: on-the-job and off-the-job techniques. The basis of differentiation is on the basis of location where the training is given; also when the method is selected to train the employee, organization keeps in mind the time and cost involved, need of employee, objectives of the organization etc.

ON-THE-JOB TRAINING (OJT) METHODS: On-the job training method is provided when the employee are taught knowledge, skills and abilities at the actual workplace. On-the-job training as takes place at the actual work station, thus the task very often contributes directly to the output of the department. The main advantages of on-the job method are that they are highly practical, and employees do not lose working time while they are learning. It includes:

- Job Instructional Technique
- Mentoring
- Coaching
- Job Rotation
- Apprenticeships And Internships
- Committee Assignment

Job Instructional Technique (JIT): This is a step by step (structured) on the job training method which has four steps which are Preparation, Presentation,

Performance and finally Follow up i.e. 3 Ps and1F in which a suitable trainer

a. Firstly the trainer prepares himself and trainee with the overview of the job, its goal, its purpose, the job, and the results desired,
b. (b)than demonstrates, or Present the task or the skills to the trainee,
c. than allows the trainee to show or perform the demonstration on his own, and
d. Finally is the follows up to provide feedback and help; here the trainee is left to perform on his own and the trainer is only their to watch and give feedbacks on the employee performance.

This method is a valuable tool for all educators (teachers and trainers). The advantages of JIT are as follows:

a. To deliver step-by-step instruction
b. To know when the learner has learned
c. To be due diligent (in many work-place environments)
d. To develop a healthy relationship between trainer and trainee.

The disadvantages of JIT are as follows:

a. Time consuming
b. Expansive as compared to others
c. Trainers are reluctant to train the trainees

- **Mentoring:** Mentoring is one of the best methods of training where an ongoing relationship is developed between a senior and junior employee, where a senior manager of the organization assumes the responsibility of grooming a junior employee. Senior manager or the trainer is called Mentor and the junior employee or trainee is called protégée or mentee especially in the defense where technical, interpersonal and political skills are generally imparted to the junior from the more experienced person. The main objective of mentoring is to help an employee attain psychological maturity and effectiveness and get integrated with the organization. Mentoring provides guidance and clear understanding of how the organization works and how it goes to achieve its vision and mission to the junior employee.

Some key Points on Mentoring

- Mentoring mainly focuses on attitude development
- It is generally conducted for management-level employees
- Mentoring is done by someone from within the organization who is well aware of the company
- It involves one-to-one interaction
- It helps in identifying weaknesses and focus on the area that needs improvement

- **Coaching:** In coaching the trainee is placed under a particular supervisor/trainer who acts as an instructor or coach and teaches job knowledge and skills to the trainee. The trainee will perform his duties assigned and coach will constantly provide feedback to the trainee. The trainee learns through performing the job and getting the feedback on the mistakes or errors. It helps in easily identifying the weak areas and tries to focus on them. The biggest problem is that it does not allow any new changes to the existing practices and styles of the trainer, and generally it is seen that the trainee may not get an opportunity to express his ideas or are reluctant to ask. This method is commonly used for training the employee in hospitality industry

- **Job Rotation:** Another type of experience-based training is job rotation, in which employees is transferred or move from job to job and from department to department in a systematic manner - in order to gain a broad understanding of the requirements of each job through cross training. It helps to develop multi/ diversified skills and a broader outlook making employee multi skilled and multitalented more suitable for growth of the employee. Also it helps to increases inter departmental co-operation and reduces monotony of work. This method is also commonly used to train the employee in hospitality industry

Some of the major benefits of job rotation are:

- Provide opportunity to broaden the horizon of knowledge, skills, and abilities of employee by working in different departments, business units, functions, and countries
- Helps to identify Knowledge, skills, and attitudes (KSAs) required
- Identification of areas where improvement is required
- Assessment of the employees who have the potential and caliber for filling the position

- **Apprenticeships and Internships:** Apprenticeships are a form of on-the-job training in which the trainee works under experienced employee for a long period of time, to teach the group of related skills that will eventually in long run will help the trainee to perform a new job or function. The trainees here serve as apprentices to experts/trainer for long periods and have to work in direct association with and also under the direct supervision of their masters so as to learn the skills. This method of training is generally seen in those trades, crafts and technical fields in which a long period is required for gaining proficiency. Apprenticeships are often used in production-oriented positions. The object of such training is to make the trainees all-round craftsmen. It is an expensive method of training where the apprentice are paid Internships are a form of apprenticeship that combines on-the- job training under a more experienced employee with classroom learning

- **Committee Assignments**: This method of training is used to improve team work among the employee. A group of trainees are asked to solve a given organizational problem by discussing the problem among them and offer solution for the problem and later the trainer will judge them.

OFF THE JOB TRAINING METHODS: Off the job training method is the learning of the employee in a place away from their actual workplace of the person. Off-the-job training has the advantage that it allows employee to get away from work and concentrate more thoroughly on the training itself. This type of training has proven more effective in inculcating concepts and ideas and has reduced the risk of breakage and errors as compared to those which happen while training at the actual workplace. It includes

- Lectures or Class Room method

- Conferences & Seminars
- Audio Visual Method
- Case Study Method
- Vestibule
- Role Playing
- Simulation

- Programmed Instruction
- Computer Based Instructions
- Sensitivity Training

Lectures or Class Room Method: Lectures and classroom methods are the traditional and direct method of explaining instructions to the employee. This method is most suitable when the numbers of trainees are more. Lectures can be very suitable in explaining the concepts and principles very clearly, and in this face to face interaction is also possible. In the colleges and universities, lectures and classrooms are the most common methods used for training.

Conference & Seminar Method: A conference is a meeting of several people and experts to discuss on any subject is called conference. Each participant contributes by analyzing and discussing various issues related to the topic. Everyone participating is free to express their own view point. It tries to explain all the necessary facts as well important principles and concepts needed to be known. Later on all the knowledge is known and shared which help in finding the solution.

Audiovisual Training: Audiovisual training methods include television, films, and videotapes etc are used to explain and train the trainee in a very time and cost effective manner. But the main drawback of audiovisual training methods is no immediate feedback or queries and they cannot be customized for a particular audience.

Case study method: The case study method is a non-directed method of study whereby trainees are provided with practical case reports to analyze. The case study includes a thorough description of any problem faced by the business which can be solved by an employee. The trainee is given a chance to analyze the case and come out with all possible solutions. Case study not only provides trainee an insight of the working of the organization but also makes them aware about the problems which are generally faced, as well as highlights the main points for future course of action thereby making them ready for future (when they will actually perform the job and will face the situation). Case Studies are basically trainee centered activities, where he is given a full opportunity to analyze the case as per his view and come out with all possible solutions, thereby helping in enhancing the analytic and critical thinking of an employee.

Vestibule Training: Vestibule Training is a term for near-the-job training, as in this workers are trained in a prototype environment, i.e. an attempt is made to create similar type of working condition just like the actual working conditions for example models or dummy etc are used to make trainee learn how to handle them so that when they actually have to handle it they are ready for it. This helps the workers to get training in the best methods and help them to get rid of initial nervousness and also helps to prevent costly mistakes on the actual machines.

Role Playing: This is one of the best and effective ways of training employees which involves realistic behavior in imaginary situation. In this a realistic role will be played by a particular trainee in an imaginary situation, each trainee takes the role of a person affected by an issue and studies. With this the person gets in to the skin of the role and portrays it creating a realistic environment. The main advantage of the role playing method is to help develop interpersonal relations and attitudinal improvisations.

Simulation: Under this method an imaginary situation is created and trainees are asked to act on it. For e.g., assuming the role of a front office manager solving the room occupancy problems or creating the new strategy etc. Simulation is any artificial environment created exactly similar to the actual situation. There are four basic simulation techniques used for imparting training to the employees: management games, case study, role playing, and in-basket training.

Programmed instructions: This type of method involves providing the necessary knowledge or the standard operating procedures to the trainees in the form of a printed text book or with printed notes or manual or some kind of teaching machine. The trainees are asked to go through it and then there are certain set of questions related to the notes which are asked from the trainee. This process of breaking down all the information into different categories making it more easy and meaningful to understand and adapt.

Computer-based training: It is the further extension of programmed instruction; Computer-based training (CBT) involves the use of computers and computer-based instructional materials as the primary medium of providing instructions to the trainee. A main benefit of CBT is that it allows employees to learn at their own pace, during convenient times. Beside that it helps in reducing the risk of damage to costly equipment by a trainee. Primary uses of CBT include instruction in computer hardware, software, and operational equipment.

Sensitivity Training: Sensitivity training is also known as T-group or laboratory training. In this method trainer tries to make trainee understand about themselves and others, this is done by developing in them social sensitivity and behavioral flexibility. It is ability of an individual to sense what others feel and think from their own point of view. In this method a group of trainees are settled in a comfortable environment and are given general topic to discuss and the trainer only act as an observer, not actively participating in the discussion, and record the behavior of each employee. It gives information about employees' his or her own personal qualities, concerns, emotional issues, and things that he or she has in common with other members of the group. It helps him to understand others view point, helps to adjust, develop team spirit.

Evaluation of Training & Development:

As we already know that organization spent huge amount in recruiting, selecting, hiring and then finally training the employee so they want to know how far the process has been useful; for this they evaluate the entire process. Evaluation involves analyzing and comparing the actual progress of the employee after training against the actual plans made by the organization, and even oriented toward improving plans for future implementation. Thus by evaluating, the organization identify whether they have been successful in training the employee or what other corrective actions can be taken. This is the last stage during the training and development process.

<u>Need for Evaluation:</u>

The purpose or need of evaluation is:

1. To identify whether the training objectives laid by the organization are accomplished or not.
2. To identify or recognize trainees who get benefited most or less from the programme.
3. To identify the cost incurred and financial benefits derive from the training programme.
4. It helps in identifying that whether the actual outcomes are aligned with the expected outcomes
5. Credibility of training and development program becomes more; when it is proved that the organization has been benefited with the process.
6. It helps in giving feedback to the candidates by defining the objectives and linking it to learning outcomes.
7. It helps in determining the relationship between acquired knowledge, transfer of knowledge at the work place, and training

<u>Evaluation Criteria:</u>

According to Hamilan evaluation of training can take place through five criteria they are;

- Reaction
- Learning
- Job Behavior
- Organization
- Ultimate Result

- **_Reactions:_** It refers to evaluating the trainee's reaction towards the training program ie his reaction towards objectives, contents and methods of training and in case trainees like the program and consider it worthwhile, the training can be considered effective.
- **_Learning:_** It refers to evaluating the trainee's ability on the basis of quantity of the content learned by them. It evaluates the degree to which trainees have learn/ mastered the concepts, knowledge and skills of the training.
- **_Job Behavior:_** This criterion of evaluation involves the manner and extent to which the trainee has applied his learning to the job. For e.g.; Improvement in his job behavior reflects the manner and extent to which he has learnt and has been applying to the job.
- **_Organization:_** This criterion of evaluation measures the use of training in the earning and changes in the behavior of the department in the form of increased productivity, quality improvement and sales turnover etc.
- **_Ultimate Results:_** It refers to the measurement of the ultimate result of the contribution of the training program to the organizational goals like survival, growth and profitability cost reduction, accident reduction, reduction in labor turnover and absenteeism etc are the best criteria for evaluating the effectiveness of training.

Methods of Evaluation: Different methods which can be used to collect and analyze the data on the outcome/result of training. Some of these are:

1. The most common method is to collect the **opinions and judgments** of trainers, superiors and peers
2. Ask the trainees to fill up **evaluation forms**
3. **Questionnaire** are given to know the reactions of trainees
4. **Oral and Written tests** are conducted to determine how far the trainees have learnt
5. **Structured Interviews** are organized with the trainees.
6. **Comparing** the **performance** of the trainees on-the-job before and after training
7. **Studying** the profiles and career development charts of the trainees.
8. **Measuring** the levels of productivity, wastage, costs, absenteeism and employee turnover after training.
9. **Comments and Reactions** of the trainee during the training period.
10. **Costs benefit** analysis of the training programme.

Limitation of Evaluation: Though the above discussion provide a broad and beautiful framework for evaluation of effectiveness of training in terms of types, levels and methods. But, it is not always possible to employee a comprehensive evaluation system due to some constraints/ limitations which are;

1. It is a Time consuming process
2. It is considered to be costly affair by the management
3. Lack of clear training policy of the organization.
4. Lack of expert trainers
5. Inadequate infrastructure
6. Unwillingness of the management to change human resource policies
7. Inadequate Performance appraisal system

8. Organizational processes have limitations

PERFORMANCE APPRAISAL - INTRODUCTION:

Performance appraisal system is used by the organizations to measure the effectiveness and efficiency of their employees by assessing their performance in a systematic manner against the standards laid by the organization, though each organization can have their own parameters of evaluating the performance of the employee but some factors against on which employee performance is evaluated are :

- job knowledge
- his skills and abilities
- his attitude towards the job
- quality and quantity of output
- initiative
- leadership qualities
- supervision
- co-operation etc.

Definitions:

According to Flippo :—Performance Appraisal is the systematic, periodic and an impartial rating of an employee's excellence in matters pertaining to his present job and his potential for a better job.

According to Heyel:—Performance Appraisal is the process of evaluating the performance and qualifications of the employees as per the requirements of the job for which he is employed, for purposes of administration including placement, selecting for promotion, providing financial rewards and other actions which require differential treatment among the members of the group as distinguished from actions affecting all members equally‖.

Thus Performance Appraisal is a formal structured and systematic method of evaluating an employee's performance and behavior so as to find out how the employee is currently performing his job and how he can perform in more effective manner in the future so that the employee, organization and society all get benefit of it.

Purpose of Performance Appraisal:

The main purposes of performance appraisal are:-

1. It help organization to clearly inform the employees about what they want from them.
2. It helps to convert organizational mission into achievable objectives.
3. It gives the insight details about the work and employees.
4. It helps to provide timely feedback to employee on their performance, thereby help employees to know where they stand in the organization in terms of their performance
5. It actually serves as the basis for promotion or job change, transfer or training of the employee depending upon the caliber and performance of employee.
6. It helps in identifying the strengths and weakness of the employees according to which HR can formulate suitable training and development program.

7. It serve as the basis for establishing the compensation – salary and wages of employee in relation to their work.
8. It helps to establish a healthy and fair environment within the organization.
9. Performance Appraisal helps in motivating and boosting the morale of employees.
10. It provides useful information to supervisors and management about their employees.
11. It increases confidence among employees.
12. It even helps to reduce overburden or overlap of job duties and ensure effective use of employee skills.
13. Performance appraisal helps to provide new ideas and information from staff.
14. It helps for skills and career development of employees.

Process of Performance Appraisal:

The Process of Performance Appraisal Includes following steps:

1. Establishing the Performance Standards

   - The performance appraisal process starts with formulating the standards or criteria, to be used for judging the performance of employees.
   - The criteria are prepared with the help of job analysis which gives the main requirements of a job and should also be discussed with the supervisors so as to ensure that all the relevant factors have been included.
   - These criteria should be clear, objective and in writing - ie who has to do the appraisal and how

frequently appraisal is to be done should also be clearly decided. Where the output can be measured the criteria is clear.

2. Communicating the Standards

    - The performance standards which are specified in the first step need to be communicated or informed and explained to the employees so that they get to know what is expected from them.

3. Measuring Performance

    - Once the performance standards are prepared and explained, the next stage is to measure the actual performance of the employee. This requires selecting the right techniques for measuring employee performance, besides that identifying the internal and external factors which have the influence on the performance of employee and finally collecting information on results achieved.

4. Comparing the Actual with the Standards

    - In the next stage actual performance of the employee collected in previous step is compared with the pre decided performance standards specified in the step 1.Such comparison will reveal the difference or the deviations which may be positive or negative. Positive deviations occur when the performance of the employee exceeds the standards. On the other hand, negative deviations suggest that excess of standard performance over the actual performance.

5. Discussing the Appraisal

·The result of the appraisal step 4 is communicated to and discussed with the employees. Not only the deviations, but also the reasons behind them are also-analyzed and discussed. Such discussion will help an employee to know his weaknesses and strengths. Therefore, he will be motivated to improve himself.

6. Taking Corrective Actions

- In the final step through mutual discussions with employees, the steps required to improve performance are identified and initiated. Training, coaching, counseling, etc. are the examples of corrective actions that help to improve performance.

Methods/Theories of Performance Appraisal:

Several methods and techniques are used for evaluating employee performance.

They may be classified into two broad categories.

A) Traditional Methods

These methods are basically the old methods of performance appraisal based on personal qualities like knowledge, capacity, capability, judgment, initiative, attitude, loyalty, leadership, etc. The following are the traditional methods of performance appraisal:

1. **Unstructured method of appraisal:**

This is a simplest method of performance appraisal. In this method, the rater or appraiser has to give his opinions about the employee. In this there is no clear specification on which parameters or qualities appraiser has to judge the common points on which raters generally rate employee are qualities, abilities, attitude, aptitude and other personal traits of the employees. This makes the method highly subjective in nature. Beside that the major drawback of the method is the higher chances of the biasness of the evaluator.

2. **Straight Ranking Method:**

It is also another one of the oldest and simplest methods of appraisal. In this technique, the evaluator gives ranks to all the employees working in the same work unit doing the same job. Employees are ranked in the order of their merit, starting from the best to the worst on the basis of overall performance. This method is also highly subjective and lacks fairness in assessing the real worth of an employee. Beside that the major drawback is that ranking of individuals having different behavior patterns or traits is difficult especially when there are large number of employees to be rated, it becomes difficult for rater.

3. **Paired Comparison Method:**

In this method the employees of a group are compared with one another at one time. It is better method of comparison than the straight ranking method, as in this method each and every employee is compared with all others in the group, one at a time ie one employee's performance is compared with that of the other employees and a decision is made on who is more competent. Then another pair is compared and the same process is repeated until all are compared and ranked. Comparison is made on the basis of overall performance.

The number of comparisons to be made can be decided on the basis of the following formula:

$$N\ (N\text{-}1)/2$$

Where N is the number of persons to be compared.

The major drawback of this method is it is not suitable for large organizations as it becomes very difficult and complex to compare large number of employees with each other.

5. **Man-to-Man Comparison Method**

In this method the performance of the employees is evaluated by obtaining ratings on his performance from the evaluators, for this a team of evaluators are involved to rate the employee. Than each rater rates employee from highest to lowest. These ratings are than used to determine the appraisal procedure for the particular employee. The benefit of this method is that employee is judged on the basis of his real performance but the drawback is that rating is given by different evaluators which may not be consistent as each evaluator has their own criteria of rating or scaling thereby making it sometimes difficult to evaluate employee performance correctly.

6. **Grading Method:**

Under this technique of performance evaluation, certain categories or factors for judging the performances are determined in advance and they are carefully defined and informed to employees. These selected and well-defined categories include:

- Grade _A' for outstanding
- Grade _B' for very good
- Grade _C' for average
- Grade _D' for poor, etc.

These grades are based on certain features such as knowledge, leadership qualities etc and the actual performance of the employee is compared with the above grades and employees allotted grades tells about their performance.

7. **Graphic Rating Scales:**

This method is perhaps the most popular and simplest technique for evaluating employee performance, in this the evaluator is asked to rate the employees on the basis of job related characteristics and knowledge of job ie, an employee's quality and quantity of work is judged on graphic scale. The factors which are taken into consideration include both the personal and related to the on-the-job characteristics. The ratings can include a scale of 1–10; excellent, average, or poor; or meets, exceeds, or doesn't meet expectations, for example. A continuous scale shows a scale and the manager puts a mark on the continuum scale that best represents the employee's performance.

The approach is multi-dimensional and very effective as several characteristics of the job are considered while evaluation. But its major disadvantage is that, ratings tend to cluster on the average side. As a supervisor often tries to rate his subordinates near to one another to avoid any criticism from them so there actual performance never comes in picture. To minimize this biasness, the raters' can be asked to give reasons to justify his rating.

8. Checklist Method:

A checklist is basically a list of objective or descriptive statements that describe the characteristics and performance of employees on the job i.e. a series of questions is asked and the rater has to simply give yes or no to the questions, which can fall into either the behavioral or the trait method, or both. Than the rater checks to indicated if the behavior of an employee is positive or negative to each statement. The performance of the employee is rated on the basis of number of positive checks.

For Ex:

- Is employee regular on the job - Yes/No
- Is employee respected by his subordinates - Yes/No
- Does the employee follow the instruction properly - Yes/No ...

Thought the checklist is the suitable method as all factors related to the job performance are considered but the major drawback is it is very much difficult to prepare a good checklist, beside that a separate checklist is needed for each job as statements used to evaluate one category of job may not be suitable for other.

9. Weighted Checklist:

The further extension of checklist method is the weighted checklist as in checklist method each statement is given equal importance wherein weighted checklist method statements or items having significant importance for organization are given weight-age thus in this method weights are assigned to different statements to indicate their relative importance like grooming, knowledge about the job, loyalty, leadership etc.

10. Free Essay Method:

In this method, no quantitative approach is used. It is open-ended appraisal of employees, where the evaluator writes a short essay on the employee's performance on the basis of his overall impression. The description given by the rater should be based on facts and should be concrete. The major drawback of this method is of biasness as evaluation is not based on specific performance dimensions of employee related to the job. Another drawback of this is that quality of appraisal depends on the writing ability of the evaluator rather than on employee performance.

11. Critical Incidents Method:

Under this method, the performance of the employee is rated on the basis of certain events that occurred during the performance of the job (i.e. the evaluation is based on key incidents). In this the evaluator rates the employee on the basis of critical events and how the employee behaved during those incidents, for this an appraiser keeps a diary to record critical incidents involving effective and ineffective job behaviors. It includes both negative and positive points. These critical incidents are later used as criteria for evaluating employee's performance

The drawback of this method is it is very time consuming and difficult for the senior to maintain a written record for each employee during every major incidents besides that critical incidents do not occur regularly therefore, a continuous record of performance might not be available.

The rater or supervisor now keeps a record of the workers their reaction and their score and at the end all the scores are added on that basis final decision is taken. Higher the score the better he employee is, but the drawback is that it is difficult for the rater to keep a record of all such incidents of large number of employee.

12. Field Review Method:

In this method, HR experts take the interviews of immediate supervisors to evaluate and judge their respective subordinates. The questions are prepared in advance which are to be asked, by the HR. By giving answers to these pre decided questions, the supervisor gives his opinions about the level of performance of his subordinate, the subordinate's work progress, his strengths and weaknesses, promotion potential, etc. The evaluator or HR takes detailed notes of the answer which are then approved by the concerned supervisor. These are then placed in the employee's personal service file. A major drawback of this method is that it is a very time consuming method. But this method helps to reduce the manager's personal biasness.

13. Confidential Reports:

This method is generally used in most government organizations. In this an annual report is prepared by the employee's immediate superior who covers the strengths and weaknesses, main achievements and failure, personality and behavior of the employee. It is highly descriptive in nature and used mainly used for promotions and transfers of employees. In this employees are not provided with the feedback. Therefore they never get the chance to know about their strengths and weaknesses. This method mainly focuses on evaluating rather than developing the employee.

14. Forced Distribution Method;

This method was developed by Tiffen to cease or stop the rater's central tendency of rating most of the employees at a higher end of the scale so as to avoid criticism. Thus in this method, the rater is forced or required to distribute his ratings in the form of a normal frequency distribution. Appraisers had to choose from among groups of statements those which best describes the employee the positive statements and those which least describes him ie the negative statements. These statements are then weighted or scored and employees with high scores are the better ones and those with low scores are the marginal ones. As the rater is not aware of what the scoring weights for each statement are, he cannot be bias and show favors to any employee.

15. Forced-Choice Method:

The forced-choice method was developed by J. P. Guilford. It contains a series of groups of statements, and rater rates how effectively the statement describes each individual who is being evaluated. Commonly forced-choice method contains two statements, both positive and negative.

Examples of positive statements are:

1. Gives good and clear instructions to the subordinates.
2. Support the team.

Examples of negative statements are:

1. Makes promises beyond his limit to keep these.
2. Inclines to favor some employees.

Each statement carries a score or weight, which is not made known to the rater. The human resource section does rating for all sets of statements— both positive and negative. The final rating is done on the basis of all sets of statements. Thus, employee rating in this manner makes the method more objective.

But the major drawback of this method is that the actual construction of several evaluative statements also called 'forced-choice scales', requires lot of time and effort.

B. MODERN METHODS

1. **Behaviorally Anchored Rating Scale (BARS):** Now days a relatively new method is being followed by organizations to judge the performance of their employees called as Behaviorally Anchored Rating Scales method (BARS) which has combine the graphic rating scale and critical incidents method to develop BARS. It is so designed to evaluate behaviors required to successfully perform a job, where each job is likely to have several job dimensions and separate scales are developed for each. It means BARS consist of predetermined critical areas of job performance or sets of behavioral statements explaining the important job performance qualities as good or bad (for e g. The qualities like inter- personal relationships, adaptability and reliability, job knowledge etc).These statements are prepared from critical incidents. Once the BARS are prepared and informed now employee's actual job behavior is judged against the desired behavior by recording and comparing the behavior with BARS.

   Though BARS standards claim that they provide better and more reliable appraisals than other methods as It utilize and combines the benefits of narratives, critical incidents, and quantified ratings by anchoring a quantified scale, but still it also has its drawbacks like developing and practicing BARS requires expect knowledge etc.

2. **Result-oriented Appraisal or MBO Technique:** This concept of Management by Objectives (MBO) was given by Peter F. Drucker in 1954 in his book. To overcome the problems of other methods, Drucker brought a new concept of management by objectives (MBO) which can be described as a —process whereby the superior and

subordinate managers of an organization jointly identify its common goals, define each individual's major areas of responsibility in terms of results expected of him and use these measures as guides for operating the unit and assessing the contribution of each its members.‖ Thus the result-oriented appraisals are based on the concrete performance targets, which are mainly established by the seniors and subordinates jointly which involves participative goal setting, choosing course of actions and decision-making, ie the employees and the seniors come together to identify and set common goals to be achieved, the standards and course of action to be taken and the criteria for measurement of their performance. It is commonly believed that as the employees themselves are involved in the goal setting and other process so they are more likely to fulfill their responsibilities.

MBO involves following four stages: goal setting, performance standard, comparison, and periodic review.

In the first stage goals are established together by the senior and the subordinates whom the employees or subordinates have to achieve. These objectives are used to evaluate the performance of the employee as they are the desired outcome to be achieved by each individual employee.

The second step is to set the standards for the employees as per the previously arranged time period. As when the employees start performing their jobs, they get to know what is to be done, what has been done, and what remains to be done.

In the third step a comparison is done between the actual performance of employees with the set standards or the goals agreed upon. Which helps the evaluator to find out the reasons for variation between the actual and standard performance of the employees? Such a comparison helps to decide the rater for the corrective actions to be taken like planning for training needs for increasing employees' performance etc.

Finally, in the fourth stage a periodic review is done to decide and initiate the corrective measures when actual performance deviates from the standards established in the first step- goal-setting stage. Periodic progress reviews are conducted in a constructive rather than punitive manner to establish new strategies for the objectives that were not met.

It is very clear from MBO stages that it is not only an effective method of performance evaluation. But it is rather viewed by the managers and employees as a philosophy of managerial practice because it is a method by which managers and subordinates plan, organize, communicate, control and debate jointly so involving active participation of all in the organization.

3. **Human Resource Accounting Method:** As already mentioned Human resources are the valuable asset for any organization. HR department is trying to measure the value of these assets in terms of money. It is believed when a competent, well trained employee leaves the organization the human asset is decreased and vice versa.

Human resource accounting method is used to find the relative worth of human assets of the organization in the terms of money. As in this method, cost of and contribution of human resources are measured and compared. Where the Cost of employees includes all the expanses organization does in terms of recruitment, selection cost, induction and placement cost, training and development cost, compensation and benefits cost etc. whereas the contributions include the benefits which employee provides through his performance ie value addition made by the employee to the organization to achieve the goals and objectives of the organization. The Difference between cost and contribution will shows the performance of employee, Ideally, the contribution of the employees should be greater than the cost incurred on them, i.e. the returns (contribution) made by the employee should be more than the money spend(Cost) on the employee, while if opposite that cost is more than the contribution made by the employee than it is the indicator for management to find out the reason for low performance, analyzing it and then taking the corrective actions. Human Resource Accounting Method is still in the transition stage.

4. **Psychological Appraisals**: These are conducted to assess the employee potential. Big Corporate Houses recruits full time psychologist to assess the future performance of the employee. Psychological Appraisals include in depth interviews, psychological tests and discussions with supervisors. It is conducted to evaluate in the following areas of employees:

   - Intellectual abilities
   - Emotional stability
   - Reasoning and analytical abilities.
   - Sociability
   - Interpretation and judgment skills
   - Motivational responses

○ Ability to foresee the future

5. **Assessment Centers:** This concept of assessment centers, to judge the performance was first used in German Army in 1930, which than gradually spread to the US and the UK in 1940s and to the Britain in 1960s. The concept gaining popularity was then used from the army to business arena during 1960s. This concept of assessment centre is of a recent origin in India, companies like Crompton Greaves, Eicher, Hindustan Lever and Modi Xerox have adopted this technique to evaluate the performance of their employees. An assessment center provides the benefit of multiple assessments of several individuals at a time performed together by the group of trained experts who uses variety of group and individual exercises to evaluate the performance of each.

In this method individuals from different departments are brought together and taken to a separate location to spend two to three days together and perform on an individual or group task similar to those they would be handling if they will be promoted. These employees are assessed by the team of senior managers along with the psychologists and the HR specialists. At the end of the process, experts give their feedback in terms of strengths and weaknesses of the each individual. The main advantage of this method is that it gives more accurate evaluation with minimum biasness, right selection and promotion of executives, etc. But still its major limitation is that the technique itself is very expansive and time consuming, causes de-motivation to the employee those who are rejected; develops unhealthy competition among the individuals, etc.

6. **360 Degree appraisal:** Another method which is gaining huge popularity these days, used for appraising the employee's performance is 360 – Degree Appraisal. This method was first developed and formally used by General Electric Company of USA in 1992. Then, it moved to other countries including India. In India, companies like Reliance Industries, Wipro Corporation, Infosys Technologies, Thomas Cook etc., have been using this method for appraising the performance of their employees.

It is a method of appraisal in which employee receive performance feedback from ―all around‖ ie from all those who are in contact with the employee in the organization – their boss, their seniors, their colleagues, their own subordinates, their customers, clients, vendors and so on. Thus, the feedback comes from all around them, - 360 degrees. It's also known as 'multi-rater feedback', as it is the comprehensive appraisal where the feedback about the employee's performance comes from all the sources which is very beneficial to the managers to provide valuable insights and information or feedback regarding the employee on his job than a traditional evaluation method of performance evaluation.

All these appraisers provide information or give feedback on an employee's skills, abilities and behaviors by filling the structured questionnaires designed for this purpose. Several parameters relating to performance and behavior are used in the questionnaires to get the overall view about the individual. All information is collected and then compiled through the computerized system to prepare individualized reports. These reports are than presented to the employee who is being rated to take future course of action.

Merit of 360 Degree Appraisal

1. It gives overall view of employee performance from all people coming in the contact of employee so it can act as an excellent tool for employee development.
2. It is more accurate, reliable and credible system as compared to others.
3. As it is a multi rated system so it is more objective in nature.
4. Individuals get a much broader perspective of how they are perceived by others than it was previously possible.

But nonetheless, like other traditional methods, it too has its weakness/demerits firstly it is time consuming and costly method and next is, this method may also suffer from the subjectivity on the part of the appraiser. For example, while supervisor not happy with employee may penalize the employee by providing negative feedback, while a peer, being influenced by _give and take feeling ie I give you good feedback, you in return will also give the same positive review to his/her colleague. Beside that it may damage the self- esteem of employees if the feedback is not good as it will be from all rounds.

The Balanced Score Card:

This system of performance evaluation was developed by Dr. Robert Kaplan and Dr. David Norton in 1992, with the aim that this system will not only measure and monitor the organizational performance but it also act as a tool which improves the communication and feedback process between the employees and management and helps to overcome the laggings of the business. In the beginning the method was used in the developed markets of the United States/Europe which later move to Asia/Australia.

As one of the main reasons for many organizations to fail or be unsuccessful, is that they fail to understand and adhere to the objectives that they have set for the organization. This balanced scorecard provides a solution for this, by breaking down objectives into simplest form and making it easier for management and employees to understand. To Plan, set targets and align strategy for the organization are two key areas where the balanced scorecard is highly beneficial.

The Balance Score Card method measures performance, by taking into consideration number of different perspectives which are – a financial perspective, a customer perspective, an internal business process perspective, and an innovation and learning perspective. With the help of these different perspectives, the BSC is able to come to conclusion in terms of both leading and lagging performance measures, thus helps in providing a more —balanced‖ view of company performance.

Leading indicators include measures, such as customer satisfaction, new product development, on-time delivery, employee competency development, etc. Traditional lagging indicators include financial measures, such as revenue growth and profitability.

Thus it suggests:

- **Financial Perspective** – It includes the costs or measurement involved, in terms of rate of return on capital (ROI) employed and operating income of the organization.

- **Customer Perspective – It me**asures the level of customer satisfaction, customer retention and market share held by the organization.
- **Business Process Perspective –** It consist of measures such as cost and quality related to the business processes.
- **Learning and Growth Perspective –** It consists of measures such as employee satisfaction, employee retention and knowledge management.

All these four perspectives are interrelated and cannot function independently, therefore organizations need one or more perspectives combined together to achieve its business objectives. For example, Customer Perspective is needed to determine the Financial Perspective, which in turn can be used to improve the Learning and Growth Perspective.

To define and assess the four perspectives, following factors are used:

Objectives –which displays the organization's objectives such as profitability or market share.

Measures – on the basis of the objectives, measures will be taken to achieve those objectives.

Targets – Next will be to set the targets to achieve those measures it could be department based or overall as a company.

Initiatives - These are basically the actions, which organization takes to meet the objectives

Importance of balanced scorecard in the organization:

- Increase the focus on the business strategy and its outcomes.
- It leads to better organizational performance through measurements.
- It helps to align the man power to meet the organization's strategy on a day-to-day basis.
- It targets the key determinants or drivers of future performance.
- It improves the level of communication in relation to the organization's strategy and vision.
- It helps to prioritize projects according to the timeframe and other factors.
- It helps to create the right balance between the components of organization's objectives and vision.
- This mechanism not only helps the management to keep a track down the performance of the organization but also helps as a management strategy.
- It helps to create a strong brand name amongst its existing and potential customers and a reputation amongst the organization's workforce.

Challenges /problems/Limitations of Performance Appraisal:

Some common challenges or problems faced by the performance appraisal system are:

a. **Halo effect**: The halo error happens due to the tendency of judging employee on one aspect, which influences the employee's overall performance ie if employee is outstanding in one area, he tends to receive outstanding or better than average ratings in other areas as well by the rater, even if such a rating is not deserved by the employee but because he has more than above on one parameter it will affects his overall performance For Example If a worker has very few absences, his supervisor might give the worker a high rating in all other areas of work because he comes on the duty regularly. Whereas, an employee might be rated high on performance simply because he has good dress sense and comes to office punctuality.

b. **Stereotyping**: Stereotyping or Negative Effect is a tendency of giving low or high rating because of mental picture that an individual holds about a person because of his age, religion, caste etc. For example, employees from rural areas might be rated poorly by raters having a sophisticated urban background, if they view rural background negatively.

c. **Central Tendency**: It a tendency of some of the raters to give average ratings to all the employees so as to avoid any kind of justification or commitment or involvement. This is done by rater so that he does not haves not to justify or clarify the average ratings. Due to which the ratings are generally seen to be clustered around the midpoint.

d. **Constant Error**: It is general tendency of some of the raters to be very lenient while rating while some others are very strict in assessing performance. Thus in the first case, performance will be overrated (leniency error) while in the second case it is underrated (strictness error). This tendency of error can be avoided by communicating the raters and explaining them clearly what is required of them.

e. **Personal Bias**: Sometimes the Performance appraisal may get affected by personal prejudices or biasness of the rater, like he may rate poorly to the employee or vice versa because the rater dislikes or likes an employee. Such biasness or prejudice by rater may arise due to regional or religious beliefs and habits or interpersonal conflicts etc.

f. **Spillover Effect or Recency**: Raters generally remember the recent performance of the employee in most cases which affects his overall performance, which for example if not good, than it will overshadows his entire year's performance this is called Recency.

g. **Lack of Reliability**: Reliability implies stability and consistency in the measurement. Lack of consistency reduces the reliability of performance appraisal. As inconsistent use of measuring standards and lack of training in appraisal techniques may also reduce reliability. Different qualities may not be given proper weightage. For example factors like initiative are highly subjective and cannot be quantified

h. **Poor appraisal forms**: Sometimes the appraisal process used by the rater might have incorrect appraisal form or method which affects the appraisal system, some common drawbacks are:

The rating scale is vague and not clear.

The appraisal form has missed the important aspects of job performance. The appraisal form may contain extra or, irrelevant performance dimensions. The forms may be too long and complex.

i. **Incompetence**: Sometimes raters themselves are not competent to judge the employee and may fail to evaluate performance accurately due to lack of knowledge and experience.

j. **Negative Approach**: Performance appraisal will also lose its value if the main focus of the management is on punishment rather than on development of employees.

k. **Multiple Objectives**: Raters may sometimes get confused due to too many objectives or unclear objectives of performance appraisal.

l. **Resistance**: Sometimes trade unions and other unions of the employee resist performance appraisal, on the basis of reason that it involves differentiation or discrimination among its members. Negative ratings by raters may affect interpersonal relations and industrial relations particularly when employees/unions do not have faith in the system of performance appraisal.

Managing Employee Performance:

The performance appraisal has always been one of the most critical areas for human resource management as it helps to manage the human resource effectively in the organization. So a proper evaluation and appraisal system can be highly valuable for the firm. Thus the researchers have undertaken the study to suggest some practical system for managing and improving employee performance in the organization which involves:

1. Set clear Goals

First and foremost step involves in effectively managing performance appraisal system is that mangers should first clearly set the objectives, goals of the organization, its expectations and communicate them properly to the employees as suggested managers should frame objectives which should be SMART:

Specific = clearly specify what is to be done, when it is to be done, who is to do the task it

And how much is to be done.

Measurable = Ask questions like: How much work is to be done? How many? How will I get to know when it is completed? for that multiple measures should be used if possible, for example, quantity, quality, time frame and cost.

Attainable = Assure the goals are reasonable and achievable and path to achieve them is feasible.

Realistic = The complexity of the objectives should needs to match with the level of employee's experience and capability ie objectives should not be beyond the control of the employee.

Time-bound = Be clear about the time frame within which performance objectives are to be achieved.

2. Monitor the performance

Once the objectives are set by the mangers and clearly communicated to the employees the next step to properly manage the performance appraisal system is to continuously and regularly monitoring the employee performance. To monitor the performance, the manger should:

- Check whether employees are able to achieve the set performance objectives
- Check whether there are any hindrance or barriers coming in the way of employee which hinder the path of employees to achieve the objectives
- Provide regular feedbacks to employee so as to achieve the set objectives of the organization
- Check if any support or changes required in the work plan or the standard set.

3. **Review**

Final step to successfully mange performance appraisal in the organization is to review the performance of the employees, which involves summarizing and highlighting the employee's performance over the course of the review period and evaluate whether they are able to achieve the desired objectives or not and what corrective actions if required should be taken .

SUMMARY:

One of the important and significant functions of HR Department is Recruitment. Recruitment is a process of searching for prospective employees and stimulating and encouraging them to apply for the job in an organization. Basically there are two sources of recruitment they are –

internal source and external sources.

Each source has their own methods of recruiting the employee with their merits and demerits. While recruiting the candidates the organization should be clear with their policies, budget, requirements so as to avoid unnecessary burden on the organization.

Training and development provide an opportunity and broad structure for the development of manpower's' technical and behavioral skills in an organization. It also helps the employee in not only attaining the organizational goal but also helps to attain personal growth. Providing training to the employee increases the skill, knowledge and talent in them. They can make themselves capable of occupying positions at higher levels. Through constant learning and development they can attain not only the technical skills but also the conceptual skills and can grow.

There are different methods of training the employee which are On the Job method –at the workplace and Off the Job –outside the workplace. Depending upon the need and other factors organization can select either of the method. But as huge cost is involved while training or developing the employee , so it becomes important for the organization to evaluate the training process that whey the organization is successful or not, so that corrective actions can be taken

Performance appraisal, also known as employee appraisal, is a method by which the performance of an employee is evaluated (generally in terms of quality, quantity, cost and time). This appraisal involves assessment of the actual performance of an employee against what is expected (standards) from him. Performance appraisals basically are a regular review of employee performance within an organization. It is a part of career development.

As such assessments are the basis of awarding promotions, effecting transfers or assessing training needs.

There are several methods of performance appraisal – traditional and modern method. To have proper performance appraisal of the employee, organizational goals should be clear and SMART and properly communicated to the employees. 360^0 degree method and the Balance score methods are latest methods of measuring the performance of employees so as to reduce the drawbacks or constraints of other methods of performance appraisal.

KEY TERMS:

Apprenticeship: A training method that puts trainees under the guidance of a master campus.

College Placements : An external search process focusing recruiting efforts on a college

Development : Activities that prepare an employees for future responsibilities.

Education : Conceptual learning that improves understanding of a subject/theme.

Employee Referral : A recommendation from a lower level position to a higher level position with increase in salary.

Executive Search : A lateral movement within the same grade, from one job to another.

Forced Choice : A method requiring the rater to select the most descriptive statement in each pair of statements about the employee being rated.

Halo Effect: Bias which occurs when the rater's personal opinion of a specific trait of employees influencing the rater's overall assessment of performance.

Job Posting: It is a method of publishing job openings on bulletin boards, electronic media and similar outlets by a company.

Job rotation: Moving a trainee from job to job to provide job training.

Knowledge : It is a familiarity with someone or something, which can include Information, descriptions, and/or skills acquired through experience or education.

MBO : An approach in which employees and supervisor jointly establish clear, Measurable performance jobs for the future.

Mentoring: an experienced employee offering guidance and support to a junior employee so that the later learns and advances in the organization.

Performance Appraisal : A systematic and objective way of evaluating both work related behavior and potential of employees.

Rating Scale: A method which requires the rater to provide a subjective performance evaluation along a scale from low to high.

Recruitment: The discovering of potential applicants for actual or anticipated organizational vacancies.

Role playing : A training method that compels trainees to assure different identities.

Selection: Picking up suitable candidate by rejecting the unsuitable.

Simulations : Any artificial environment that tries to closely mirror an actual condition.

Skill : A skill is the learned capacity to carry out predetermined results often with the minimum outlay of time, energy, or both. These includes case studies, decision games, role plays etc.

Training: Activity that teach employees how to perform their current jobs.

Vestibule : A training method involving the creation of training facilities separate from the regular production area but with the same equipment.

THREE

EMPLOYEE MOTIVATION, COMPENSATION AND BENEFIT MANAGEMENT

INTRODUCTION:

Human beings in their day to day life get engage in various types of actions for example a When you come from school; you feel hungry and want to eat something. You want to eat because there is a force which compels you to have food. A man is working hard to get the job and so on, behind each of these actions, there is a driving force which is compelling you to engage in that action this is called motivation for example you eat because you are hungry, or man is working hard to get the job because he wants to earn money etc. This basic answer of this question is 'why of behavior' or factors which compel us to do certain activities make us study the psychological process called motivation.

Compensation is basically that which an employee receives, in exchange of his contribution to the organization. If the employee is satisfied with the compensation plan of the organization, he will be highly motivated and satisfied with the organization thereby increasing the productivity of the organization. Although there can be monetary and non monetary forms of compensation, it is the monetary compensation which is the most basic element by which employees are attracted, motivated satisfied toward their work and organization.

MOTIVATION - INTRODUCTION:

The word Motivation is derived from the Latin word _mover', meaning, _to move'. It is the driving force which causes action among the individuals. It can be referred as an act of stimulating someone or oneself to get desired course of action. Motivation is basically the willingness to do something, and is conditioned by this action's ability to satisfy some need for the individual. Motivation is the

Definitions:

According to Scott —Motivation means a process of stimulating people to action to accomplish desired goals".

As defined by Latham & Ernst, 2006, motivation has been defined as —a psychological process resulting from the reciprocal interaction between the individual and the environment that affects a person's choices, effort, and persistence‖

Motivation can also be defined as —The processes that account for an individual's intensity, direction, and persistence of effort toward achieving a goal‖

- Intensity shows how hard an employee tried
- Direction shows how employee intensity towards work should benefit the organization (i.e. quality of effort counts)
- Persistence shows for how long employee can maintain his/her effort?

Concept of Motivation:

The term motive usually is explained as desires, needs, emotions or impulses that make someone do something following this definition, motivation is the state of being incited to action. It is actually a process that starts with a physiological or psychological need which activates a behavior or a drive within the individual which is aimed towards the goal. Then we initiate an action to achieve that goal and if we take into consideration work environment it crystal clear that work motivation refers to motivation within a work setting. Typically, it refers to employee motivation to perform, stay and committed towards the organization, cooperate, lead or support a leader, help customers etc. Thus it is very clear fact that if leaders want their employees to perform efficiently and effectively they need to keep their employee motivated so that they work towards achievement of the organizational goals.

As proved motivated employees are an asset for an organization, they are directly proportional to an organization's success, if employees are motivated they will work efficiently towards achieving the organizational objectives. Motivation is intangible, difficult to measure and extremely difficult to control, but very easy to facilitate if done right. It's all about intention, intensity, and perseverance.

Importance or Need of motivation: Motivation offers several importance's to the organization and to the employees:

Motivation is important to an individual as:

- Motivation will help him achieve his personal goals.
- If an individual is motivated, he will have job satisfaction.
- Motivation will help in self-development of individual.
- An individual would always gain by working with a dynamic team.
- Effective coordination among employee
- Loyalty and commitment comes with the motivation.

Similarly, Motivation is important to a business as:

- The more motivated the employees are, the more empowered the team is.
- The more is the team work and individual employee contribution, more profitable and successful is the business.
- During period of amendments, there will be more adaptability and creativity.
- Motivation will lead to an optimistic and challenging attitude at work place.

1. Reduces absenteeism and labor turnover

2. Helps to improve the image of the organization
3. Promotes harmony in the organization

Types of Motivation:

Motivation can be classified into two on the basis of the place from where the need arises, they are:

- Intrinsic motivation
- Extrinsic Motivation

Intrinsic Motivation: It is a type of motivation in which the motives originates from inside or within the human body. It refers to the internal driving state stimulating an individual to behave in a specific way. As individuals are motivated from within, such employee's have the desire to perform well at the workplace because the results are according to the employee's/her belief system. Such type of motivational force are usually the strongest motivational factor motivating the employee so such type of employee will show qualities like acceptance, curiosity, honor, desire to achieve success.

It commonly includes following motives:

- Biological drives such as hunger, thirst relief from pain etc
- Curiosity
- Internal fears like fear of rejection
- Psychological needs like need for being accepted or appreciated etc
- Internal desires like desire to gain power

Extrinsic Motivation: This type of motivation originates from outside the human body, the driving force exits outside the human body that initiates the human for actions. Such type of employee are motivated with external factors like rewards and recognition and would never be motivated internally and only external motivation would act on them to get the tasks done.

The common motives are:

- Incentives
- Bonus
- Allowances
- Promotion and demotions
- Rewards and punishment etc

Motivational Theories:

There are many theories available, to explain the nature of motivation. These theories are fully or, at least, partially true, and all tries help to explain the behavior of people or employee at certain times. However, the search for a generalized theory of motivation is still continued It is all because of the complexity of nature of motivation and the fact that there is no single reply to what motivates people to work well, as each individual is different and so their motivational factor is also different thus these different theories are important for the managers to guide them. They show that there are many motives, which influence people's behavior and performance. The different theories of motivation are usually divided into two approaches: content theories and process theories.

Content Theory-Content theories include all those specific things, which actually motivate the employee at work. Thus content theories place emphasis on *what* motivates.

Process Theory -A process theory tries to identify the relationship among the dynamic variables, which make up motivation. These theories are more concerned with how behavior is initiated, directed and sustained. Thus process theories place emphasis on the actual process of motivation.

Content Theory includes:

Maslow's Need Hierarchy Theory: The well known and pioneering theory of motivation is of Maslow's-Hierarchy of Needs Theory. This theory was developed by Abraham Maslow and is based on the assumption that people are motivated by a series of five universal needs as shown in Fig 3.1. These needs are ranked, according to the order in which they influence human behavior, i.e. in hierarchical order from bottom to top.

These needs are:

- **Physiological needs** are considered to be the lowest and the basic needs of individual. These needs include the needs such as food, water, shelter and clothes etc. Till the time person's physiological **needs are unsatisfied, they exist as a driving or motivating force** in a person's life.
- Once the physiological **needs are satisfied than the next need a person think of is Safety needs** which include the needs for shelter and security they become the motivators of human behavior. A desire for security, stability, dependency, protection, freedom from fear and anxiety, and a need for structure, order, and law. In the workplace this needs translates into a need of job

security, medical security; safe work environment, proper compensation etc.

- Next is the **Social needs which** include the need for belongingness and love. Every individual wants acceptance by the group, society, friendships, love etc. In the workplace, this need may be satisfied by an ability to interact with peers, subordinates and even seniors and perhaps to be able to work collaboratively with all.

  - After the social needs have been satisfied, **ego and esteem needs** become the motivating needs of individual. Esteem needs include the desire for self-respect, self-esteem, recognition by others, feeling of achievement and the esteem of others. In workplace, these needs include the desire for reputation, prestige, status, fame, glory, dominance, recognition, attention, importance, and appreciation.
  - The highest need in Maslow's hierarchy is that of **self-actualization**; the need for self-realization, continuous self-development, and the process of becoming all that a person is capable of becoming i.e. fulfillment of capacities.

In brief Maslow needs theory can be summarized as:

1. Physiological needs - (food, clothing, shelter, etc,)
2. The need for safety and security - (freedom from danger, job security, health care etc)
3. Social need or need to belong - (Acceptance by the group, friendships, love etc,)
4. Esteem need - (Recognition by others, feeling of achievement etc)
5. Self-actualization needs - (fulfillment of capacities)

The needs in Maslow hierarchy are arranged in order of their importance in the hierarchical pyramid from lowest need at the bottom to highest need at the top, with the assumption that a lower level need will be satisfied first, before the person will move to the next higher level need which now becomes a motivating factor. People try to satisfy their physiological needs first. When their basic needs are ensured, they desire for security, belongingness, esteem and finally self- actualization.

Alderfer's Theory of Motivational Need: Clayton **Alderfer** reworked on Maslow's Need Hierarchy and reorganized Maslow need hierarchy theory into three levels of core needs. Alderfer's theory is called the **ERG theory** -- Existence, Relatedness, and Growth.

- **Existence need** refers to the concern for basic materials required for the existence of the persons; which were called - physiological and safety needs by Maslow theory. Thereby Existence needs includes both physiological and safety need of Maslow corresponding the lower-order needs of Maslow's theory.

- **Relatedness need** refers to the desire that individual have for love and belongingness and maintaining interpersonal relationships; similar to Maslow's social/love need, and the external component of his esteem need.

Growth need refers to an intrinsic desire for personal development; it include Maslow's intrinsic components of esteem need, and self-actualization needs. Relatedness and growth needs together comprise the higher order needs of

Maslow.

Alderfer's ERG theory differs from Maslow's Need Hierarchy theory as ERG theory explained that **more than one need may be operative at the same time - a higher and lower need may be operating together on an individual ie** multiple needs can be operating as motivators at the same time contrast to Maslow that only need can motivate person at one time, once achieve than the person will move for next. Even ERG theory **does not assume that there exist a rigid hierarchy** where a lower need must be substantially satisfied before one can move on.

Another difference as suggested was- according to Maslow an individual would stay at a certain need level until that need is not satisfied. ERG theory counters it by suggesting that when a higher- order need level is not satisfied; the individual's desire to satisfy a lower- level need increases. For example inability to satisfy a need for social interaction (social need), might increase the desire for more money or better working conditions (psychological need).

McClelland's Theory of Needs: David McClelland and his associates, focused on needs similar to the higher order (social and esteem) needs identified by Maslow. McClelland's needs theory, also called Achievement motivation theory is basically concerned with how individual needs and environmental factors combine to form three basic human motives.

- achievement
- affiliation
- influence

Need for Achievement (nAch) : The need for achievement is characterized by people who wish to take responsibility for finding solutions to problems, master complex tasks, set goals, get feedback on level of success, who like challenges, and are willing to work hard to reach the ultimate goal.

Need for Affiliation (nAff) : The need for affiliation is characterized by people who desire for affection and establishing friendly relationships, to belong, an enjoyment of teamwork, a concern about interpersonal relationships, and a need to reduce uncertainty.

Need for Power (nPow): The need for power is characterized by a people who wish to control and influence others, a need to win arguments, a need to persuade and prevail, need to be influential, and to control others. Individuals with this type of need are concerned with acquiring the full control and power in their hands.

According to McClelland, the presence of these motives or drives in an individual indicates why an individual behaves in certain ways.

Herzberg's Two Factor Theory: It is also known as the **Motivation-Hygiene Theory, and was developed by** Frederick Herzberg and his associates. On the basis of interviews taken from around 200 engineers and accountants employed in different industries in an around Pittsburgh area, U.S.A. developed a Two factor model of motivation. In the interviews they were asked about what kind of things on their job made them happy or satisfied and what things on job made them unhappy or dissatisfied.

After the analysis they found that there are two factors to which an organization can adjust to influence the levels of motivation at the workplace. They are motivating factors and Hygiene factors.

Motivating Factors/ Motivators (Satisfaction): Those factors of the job which provide satisfaction or contentment to the employee, they feel happy about it are called Motivators. Some of them are: achievements, recognition, advancement, work itself, responsibility, growth etc. The presence of motivators leads to satisfaction in the job, whereas the absence of it will prevent both satisfaction and motivation.

Hygiene Factors (Dissatisfaction): These are those factors of the job which if not present will discourage employees from doing their best at work. According to Herzberg these are those factors which if present will prevent dissatisfactions but do not increase satisfaction or motivation while the absence of which, increase dissatisfaction from the job. They are Company policies and administration, supervision, working conditions, security, status, salary, interpersonal relations are known as Hygiene factors. As presence of hygiene factors will prevent dissatisfaction from the job so he called these factors as dis-satisfiers / maintenance factors.

This can be further explained with an example: Suppose a manager who tries to reduce or eliminate factors that can create job dissatisfaction in the job, this as found can only bring peace from the job but not necessarily motivation among employees. They will only be able to pacify their employees rather than motivating them. That is why if things like quality of supervision, pay, company policies, physical working conditions relations with others and job security etc are properly present in the workplace / organization, employees will not be dissatisfied ; but they will neither be satisfied.

Thus if we want to motivate our employees and wants growth of the organization, Herzberg suggested to give emphasis on those factor which act as a motivators for the employees likes promotional opportunities, opportunities for personal growth, recognition, responsibility and achievement etc.

Reinforcement Theory: It is also called as Organizational Behavior Modification Theory or O.B. Model. This model was developed by B.F Skinner is based on the behaviouristic approach and very much different from other cognitive theories of motivation. As in cognitive theories like Maslow's need hierarchy –Internal needs of an individual became the cause of action or lead to behavior by the employee, while reinforcement theory suggest that external consequences only tend to determine behavior of individual. It completely ignores the inner state of needs of the individual.

Reinforcement theory further suggested that human behavior can be described in terms of the previous positive or negative outcomes of that behavior. Those behaviors, which were previously rewarded, will be repeated in future with an aim to be rewarded again while those behaviors, which were previously either not rewarded or instead were punished, tend to disappear or will not be repeated. Thus behavior modification is based on the idea that individual behavior depends on its consequences and therefore, it is possible to control a number of employee behaviors by manipulating their consequences.

Skinner believed that person's behavior can be controlled and shaped by reinforcing desired behavior consecutively and continuously. As and when the reinforced behavior is repeated, the unrewarded behavior tends to disappear. If the behavior is not the same as desired by a superior, repeated reinforcements in the desired direction can be provided to move the actual behavior close to the desired behavior. Thus reinforcement method provides a strong and powerful mode of shaping behavior.

Rewards or reinforcements should meet an employee's specific needs and must be applied equitably. Management should have a very clear idea about the behavior they want from their employees to encourage and consistent in reinforcing them.

Adam's Equity Theory: This theory was developed by J. Stacy Adams and is based on the principle of balance or equity that people want to be treated fairly. This theory sates that level of motivation in an individual is related to his or her perception of equity and fairness managed by management. Greater the fairness followed by management, higher the motivation and vice versa. To assess the level of fairness, employee makes comparison of input in the job (in terms of contribution) with that of outcome (in terms of compensation) and compares the same with that of another colleague of same rank.

In simple terms, this theory states that equity occurs when according to individual ratio of a his outcome to his inputs equals to the ratio of another person's output to inputs and inequity occurs when a person perceives that the ratio of his outcomes to inputs and the ratio of a other's outcomes to inputs are unequal. The inputs includes: education, social status, qualifications, age, organizational positions etc and outputs includes: rewards such as pay, promotion, the intrinsic interest in the job etc, of a person and other and are based up on the person's perceptions. Equity theory assumes that employees assess their performance and attitudes by making a comparing between both their contribution and the benefits they derive from work to the contributions and benefits of another person.

Thus the theory recognizes that individuals are not only concerned with the amount of rewards they get for their efforts, but also with that of amount received by other. Equity theory further tells that individuals are motivated to reduce any perceived inequity. They will work to make the ratios of outcomes to inputs equal. To eliminate this inequity, the person comparing will work to make the ratios equal by changing either the outcomes or the inputs, so as to return to the condition of equity.

This process theory of motivation is also not free from criticism. Firstly it is difficult to assess the perception of employees. Secondly it is quite difficult to choose another comparable person...

Motivating Employees:

There are several motivational factors that motivate a person to work. The motivational factors can be broadly classified into two groups:

I. **MONETARY FACTORS**: It includes

a. **Salaries or wages**: Salaries or wages are one of the most important motivational factors. Reasonable salaries as according to the nature of the job should be given to employees and that too should be paid on time. While fixing salaries the organization must consider factors such as:

  - Cost of living
  - Company ability to pay
  - Capability of company to pay etc,

b. **Bonus:** It means an extra payment given to an employee over and above salary given as an incentive. The employees must be given proper amount of bonus.

c. **Incentives**: Most of the organizations now a day's provide additional incentives such as medical allowance, educational allowance, HRA , allowance, etc. to motivate their employees.

Some organization also provide:

d. **Special individual incentives**: Such incentives are given to deserving employees for giving valuable suggestions for the growth of the organization.

II. **Non Monetary factors**: It includes:

a. **Status or job title**: Not only money instead by providing a higher status, rank or designations to the employee can also be use to motivate the employee. Employees prefer and are proud of their higher designations.

b. **Appreciation and recognition**: The appreciation and recognition not only coming from immediate superior but also from higher authorities can motivate employee and should be done at regular intervals.

c. **Delegation of authority**: Delegation of authority motivates a subordinate to perform the tasks with dedication and commitment. When authority is delegated, the subordinate knows that his superior has placed faith and trust in him.

d. **Proper Working conditions**: A healthy safe and harmonious work environment can itself be a source of motivation for the employee.

e. **Job security**: Guarantee of job security or lack of fear dismissal, etc can also be a good source of motivation of the employees.

f. **Workers participation**: Allowing the employee to be a member of quality circle, or a committee, or some other form of employee participation can also motivate the work-force.

g. **Providing training to the employees:** creating environment to provide training to the manpower so as to help him to enhance his knowledge, skills and abilities so that he not only become efficient for the organization but also helps in his overall development of employee.

h. **Flexible working hours**: a new concept of flexible working shifts has now been introduced to allow employee to maintain work life or work home balance.

i. **Cordial** relations between management and employees

Beside monetary and non monetary factors, management can plan for things at the level of job for motivating employees that can be:-

j. **Job Design**: It means designing the jobs in such a manner that create both a challenging and interesting task for the employee and is effective and efficient in motivating the employee and for getting the job done. Four approaches to job design are:

i. **Job Simplification:** The goal of this job design approach is to standardize and specialize tasks. But the drawback of this approach is that, it does not always helps to increase motivation as the jobs can become boring.

ii. **Job Enlargement:** The goal of this job design approach is to combine two to three tasks together and making it large, to give the employee a greater variety of work.

iii. **Job Rotation:** The goal of this job design approach is to move workers to different tasks periodically so that they can learn other task also and can become multi- skilled.

iv. **Job Enrichment:** Job enrichment involves introducing more challenging tasks and responsibilities to the employee. For example if an supervisor who is involved in preparing and presenting reports of performance, can also be asked to frame plans.

All these and several other methods can be adopted to keep employees motivated so that perform their task effectively and efficiently this well not only help in overall development and growth of organization but also of the employee himself. While planning the approach to motivate the employee HR must keep this in mind that each individual is different from each other and one method of motivation can not necessarily be effective for all.

Measurement:

To measure employee motivation is a difficult task as motivation is a qualitative in nature, rather than quantitative, value i.e. it cannot be easily measured and described in numbers or statistics. Though it is difficult to measure but it is not an impossible task as those organizations that use targets and sales incentives, can often calculate the motivation of their employees with the use of surveys and questionnaires interview etc methods, directed to the employee and the customer.

The methods employed for the measurement of motives may be:

A) Conduct Survey: The surveys can be done to know the real motivational level of the employee by providing questionnaires to the employees, by answering these questionnaires; the employees will try to show their feelings and attitude towards the different conditions related to their work i.e. what they feel about their job, and all aspects related to the job. The next job of the HR is to collect these questionnaires and analyze them. Analysis of their replies will guide the management towards the level of motivation or morale of the employee towards the work and the organization as a whole, as well as the analysis will also help the HR to find the likes and dislikes of the employee in the prevailing employment situation and what can be done to raise the morale of different employee as each employee is different and his level of motivation will also be different.

Interviews: Another most frequently used method to judge the morale of the employee is through interview. By frequent and periodic interviews with employees the morale of them is assessed. During the interview session, the interviewer or HR encourages the employee to speak honestly and freely about the job, his task job, his supervisors, his fellow employees, and any other conditions affecting his employment without any fear or hazard to his status in the organization. Though this method is very effective but its drawback is that the employees are reluctant to give honest reply

Indirect Method: Some other methods which can also be used to judge the level of morale of the employee is by the use of comment cards, feedback forms etc to be filled by the guest about the employee (more suitable in service industry) if the card is positive about the employee which suggest the employee is highly motivated and like his job while vice versa as a highly motivated employee will most likely result in more satisfied customers, than that of an employee with less motivation. Organizations can also use checklist method to judge the level of motivation of employee

Though organizations can use different method to evaluate the level of morale of employee but each method have their own limitations and drawbacks as motivation is not purely quantitative in nature.

COMPENSATION - INTRODUCTION:

Compensation is a systematic approach to provide monetary value to employees in exchange of the work performed by the employee. Employee compensation may achieve several purposes in recruitment, job-performance and job satisfaction. Good compensation plans have salutary effect on the employee. As if they are happy with the compensation plan, they are satisfied, devoted towards the organization and thereby increasing the productivity of the organization.

Definition: —Employee compensation refers to all forms of pay given to employees which arises from their employment". It can also be defined as 'all the rewards earned by employees in return for their labor or hard work'.

Another definition suggest that —Compensation is defined as the total amount of the monetary and nonmonetary pay provided to an employee by an employer in return for their work performed as required by the organizationl.

It can also be defined as – 'Compensation includes direct cash payments, indirect payments in the form of employee benefits & incentives to motivate employees to strive for higher levels of productivity'.

Concept - Compensation:

As compensation is the total cash and non-cash payments that an organization give to his employee in exchange of the work they do for your business. It is typically one of the biggest expenses made by the businesses with employees, so in order to have consistent pay across equivalent positions, it becomes necessary for the management to first know what the work of each position is (Job description) and then decides which work is, in fact, equal. This will help in the course of preparing and maintaining a position classification plan as well as deciding the compensation of each employee. In addition to this managers have to observe several external formalities like political, social, legal, etc that offer physical as well as financial security to employees. All these issues will play a major role towards the HR Department efforts to obtain, maintain and retain an effective workforce

Nature of compensation: Employees provide their services to the organization with an aim or attraction to receive three types of rewards which include-

Base Pay: which refers to the base wages and salaries, it is the basic compensation an employee normally receives from the organization.

Variable Pay: it is in the form of Incentives which include bonuses, commissions and profit sharing plans, which are so designed to encourage employees to perform better than the normal expectation. It is the compensation linked directly to performance of the employee, better the performance and productivity, more will be the incentives.

Benefits: These are indirect type of compensation or rewards given to an employee or group of employees as a part of organizational membership like health insurance, vacation pay, retirement pension etc.

Objectives & Importance of Compensation Plan:

Objectives of Compensation Management: The following are the objectives of compensation management:

- To pay people as according to their worth
- To pay or reward employee according to what the organization values and wants to pay for.
- To reward people for the outcome/value they create.
- Reward the right things to convey the right message about what is important in terms of outcomes and behaviors.
- To develop a performance culture.
- To motivate employees and obtain their commitment and engagement towards the organization.
- Help to attract and retain the high quality people as per the need of the organization needs.
- Create total reward system which includes the importance of both financial and non financial rewards.
- Align reward practices with both business goals and employee values.

Importance of effective Compensation Plan: Compensation is used to:

- Recruit and retain qualified employees.
- Attract and Retain talent
- Ease in Operations
- Helps in cost control
- Increase Productivity
- Comply with Legal rules
- Increase or maintain morale/satisfaction.
- Reward and encourage peak performance.
- Achieve internal and external equity.
- Reduce turnover and encourage company loyalty.
- Modify (through negotiations) practices of unions.

Basis for classifying components of compensation:

Compensation is primarily the only HR activity which has its major impact on all other functions of organization regarding personnel and compensation will be considered fair by employees if it is based on systematic components. Various compensation systematic components have been developed to determine the value of positions:

The different basis for classifying components of a compensation system is:

Job Analysis: It is the process of analyzing a job on the basis of which job descriptions and job specifications are developed. Job analysis techniques include the use of interviews, questionnaires, and observation

Job Descriptions: It is a critical component of both compensation and selection systems, Job description basically define in writing the duties and responsibilities of employee, job requirements, functions, duties, location, environment, conditions, and other aspects of jobs. Descriptions can be developed either individually for each job or for entire job families.

<u>Job Evaluation</u>: A system used for comparing jobs for the purpose of identifying appropriate compensation levels for individual jobs or job elements. There are four main techniques: Ranking Classification, Classification, Factor Comparison, and Point Method.

Pay Structures: It is used for standardizing compensation practices. Most pay structures include several grades with each grade containing a minimum salary/wage and either step increments or grade range. Step increments are common with union positions where the pay for each job is pre-determined through collective bargaining.

Salary Surveys: It includes collections of salary and market data which may include average salaries, inflation indicators, cost of living indicators, salary budget averages. Organizations can either purchase the results of surveys conducted by survey vendors or they may themselves conduct their own salary surveys. When purchasing the results of salary surveys conducted by other vendors, ensure that surveys may be conducted within a specific industry or across industries as well as within one geographical region or across different geographical regions. Try to know from which industry or geographic location the salary results data collected before comparing the results to your company.

Policies and Regulations: Compensation will be perceived as fair if it is made up of a system of components developed to maintain internal and external equity.

Components of Compensation:

Compensation system should be designed in such a manner that it should be able to attract, retain and motivate employees. Total payable compensation or special benefits can be paid in different forms.

Besides classifying components of compensation in many other ways, one method of classification that has been discussed is *'financial compensation and non-financial compensation'*.

Financial components include:

1. Basic wage/salary
2. Dearness allowance
3. Bonus
4. Incentive compensation
5. Fringe benefits

Basic Wages/Salaries: Basic wages / salaries are the main cash components of the wage structure; on the basis of them other elements of compensation are structured. It is generally a fixed amount which can be changed due to annual increments or due to periodical pay hikes. Salary represents the monthly rate of pay given to white collar employee and wages represent hourly rates of pay given to blue collar employee. The amount will differ from employee to employee, and depend upon the nature of job, seniority, and merit and are subjected to annual increments.

Dearness Allowance (DA): It is the allowance paid to employees in order to enable them to face the increasing dearness of essential commodities. This payment of dearness allowance helps the employees and workers to face challenges of the increase in price or inflation of prices of goods and services consumed by them. The amount of dearness allowance is fixed percentage on the basic wage, and instead of increasing the wages every time, DA is paid to neutralize the effect and helps the employees to face the challenges.

Incentives: Incentives are also called as _payments by results' are the extra earnings or are paid in addition to wages and salaries due to the excellent performance by the employee or group, targets achieved , increase in productivity , sales, profit or cost reduction efforts. These are given to motivate the employee as well as it helps to encourage other employees also to work hard and gain the incentives

There are:

- Individual incentive schemes
- Group incentive programmes

Individual incentives are given to specific employee for his extraordinary performance. While

If there is a group task or any work, incentives are paid collectively to the group , which they can divide among group members on an equitable basis

Bonus: The bonus amount can be decided and paid in different ways by the management. Bonus can be a fixed percentage on the basic wage paid annually or in proportion to the profitability. Even the Government has also mentioned a minimum statutory bonus for all employees and workers. There is also a bonus plan which compensates the managers and employees based on the sales revenue or profit margin achieved. Bonus plans can also be based on piece wages but depends upon the productivity of labor.

Fringe Benefits: Fringe benefits include a wide range of benefits and services that employees receive as an important part of their total compensation package, based on the critical job factors and performance. Fringe benefits are basically the indirect compensations given to the employees due to the condition of employment, under which employee work and are not directly related to the performance of concerned employee. Fringe benefits act as a supplement to regular wages received by the workers from the employers

These benefits given to the employees can be easily calculated but the amount of benefit is generally not predetermined and the main purpose of providing fringe benefit is to retain efficient and capable employee making them loyal towards organisation which also act as a security base for employee.

They include benefits such as paid vacation, pension, health and insurance plans, etc.

Non Financial Compensation

It includes:

- Non monetary benefits
- Leave Policy
- Overtime Policy
- Hospitalization
- Insurance
- Leave travel
- Retirement Benefits
- Holiday Homes.
- Flexi Timing

Non-Monetary Benefits: It is not always possible to provide monetary benefits to employees to keep their morale high so in such situations non monetary benefits are offered to employees, these benefits helps in providing psychological satisfaction to employees even when financial benefits are not available.

Such benefits are:

a. Recognition of merit through certificate
b. Offering challenging job responsibilities
c. Promoting growth prospects
d. Healthy and harmonious working conditions
e. Minimizing supervision
f. Involvement in decision making etc

Leave Policy: It is the right of every employee working to get proper number of leave while working with the organization. The commonly provided paid leaves by the organizations are casual leaves, medical leaves (sick leave), and maternity leaves, statutory pay, etc.

Overtime Policy: There should a written down policy for overtime so as to motivate employees to work extra or overtime for which they should be provided with the adequate allowances and facilities during their overtime.

Hospitalization: The organizations should also provide allowances to employees to get their regular medical check-ups, even their dependents should also be eligible for the mediclaims this help in providing them emotional and social security.

Insurance: Organizations also provide accidental insurance and life insurance for employees to give employees mental and emotional security as well as to make them feel valuable for the organization.

Leave Travel: The employees are nowadays also given leaves and travel allowances to go for holiday with their families. This is provided to give relaxation time to employees. Some organizations even arrange tour for their employees.

Retirement Benefits: Organizations provide pension plans and other benefits to their employees to support employees even after they retire from the organization at the prescribed age.

Holiday Homes: Some organizations are now days providing holiday homes and guest house for their employees at different locations. These holiday homes are provided so that employees can relax and enjoy as well as work as well as help during transfer of employee from one destination to other.

Flexible Timings: Now day's organizations also provide flexible work timings to those employees who cannot come to the work during the normal shifts due to their personal problems and valid reasons.

Employee Benefits:

To motivate and keep their employees satisfied, the organization or HR Department not only provide salaries, bonus, perquisites, etc., but also provide them with different financial and non financial benefits like old age benefits, retirement benefits, voluntary retirement benefits etc., This also play a important role in selecting the work, organization, job by the employees and helps to retain and motivate employees at different organizations. Some of the monetary and nonmonetary benefits are mentioned above also, beside that some other special benefits provided by the organization to retain and motivate their employees are:

Gratuity: Gratuity is the huge or large sum of amount offered as the retirement benefit to the employees for their long and continuous service. —It is a lump sum payment given to a worker or to his family by the employer on termination of his service due to retirement, retrenchment, invalidity or death. This helps the employee to survive his living even after retirement from the organization.

The Payment of Gratuity Act, 1972 was passed as Act No. 30 of 1972 and received the assent of the President of India on 21 August, 1972. It was enforced with effect from 16 September, 1972.

Voluntary Retirement Scheme (VRS): It is also called as Golden Handshake, where Voluntary Retirement means to voluntarily or willingly ceasing/finishing the job before the actual time period due to any reason, it is legally tenable and is an integral part of public policy.

Disability Benefits: When employees are not able to work because of some accident or some health-related issues, this refers to disability to work, disability may be classified as regular, temporary total, or partial. Then it becomes the ethical and social responsibility of the management of the organization to provide disability benefits or disability income to the employees to overcome the problem they are facing; continuity in the payments can help the employee to maintain their existing lifestyle without much major changes.

Various disability income benefits provide weekly or monthly payments in relation to the organization policy. The major components are as follows:

1. Short-term disability
2. Long-term disability
3. Workers compensation

4. Non-occupational disability
5. Social security
6. Travel accident insurance
7. Accidental death and dismemberment
8. Group life insurance: Total permanent Disability (TPD)
9. Sick leave
10. Supplemental disability insurance
11. Retirement plans.

Deferred Income: With the growth of industrialization, trade unions, increase in government interference in industrial sectors, employers have established various kinds of compensation components to help employees accumulate capital and meet future financial goals:

1. Social security
2. Qualified Retirement Plan

    a. Pension plan
    b. Profit-sharing plan
    c. Stock bonus plan

3. Simplified employee Pension Plans(SEPs)
4. Supplemental executive Retirement Plans(SERPs)
5. Supplemental and executive group life Insurance Plans
6. Stock purchase Plan
7. Stock Option Plan
8. Stock Grant

Spouse and family income protection: Most employee try to ensure that there should be a secured future of their dependents or family members in case of their death i.e. incase of their untimely death there should be some benefits provided to their dependent who can live their life with the help of that benefit received.

One component, ie - life insurance is already there, beside that there are several components which have a specific features to help the worker's dependents in such a calamity situation.

Some of the major components available to protect worker's dependents are:

1. Life Insurance
2. Social Security and Medicare
3. Tax – sheltered Annuity
4. Workers' Compensation
5. Retirement plans
6. Accidental death and Dismemberment
7. Travel Accident Insurance
8. Healthcare Coverage.

Health and Accident Protection: Organizations also provide their employees with different variety of insurance services to help them and their families to maintain a normal standard of living when unusual or unexpected health-related adversities occur. These healthcare-related insurance plans cover medical, Surgical, and hospital bills resulting from an accident or illness. This helps the employees and their families to fight against the unnatural calamities happening.

Time-Off with Pay: Many organizations now days also provide the time-off with pay such as Leave Travel Allowances, Home Travel Allowances, and Special Leave with holiday packages, etc.

Factors affecting wages or compensation or determinants of wages or compensation:

As already mentioned above that the **Compensation** involves huge expanse from the organization for the employee thus it becomes important for the HR Department that before deciding the compensation of the employee, should take into consideration several factors.

INTERNAL FACTORS: The internal factors exist within the organization and influences the pay structure of the company. These are as follows:

- **Ability to Pay:** It suggest that amount of salary/wages of employee depends upon the employer's ability to pay salary/wages to the employee, which depends upon the profitability of the firm. This means that prosperous or big companies can pay higher compensation as compared to their competitors while the smaller companies can afford to pay scale up to the level of competitors or sometimes even below the industry standards.

- **Business Strategy:** The strategies of the organization also affect the employee compensation. In case if the company wants to have the skilled workers, so as to be above the competitor, they will offer more pay as compared to the others. Whereas, if the company wants to go smooth and is managing with the available workers, will give relatively less pay or equivalent to what others are paying.

- **Job Evaluation and Performance Appraisal:** The job evaluation helps to have a satisfactory differential pays for the different jobs. The performance Appraisal helps an employee to earn extra on the basis of his performance. If they perform well they will get increased compensation thereby they get motivated and perform their job more efficiently.

Employee: The employee or a worker himself influences the compensation in one of the following ways:

- Through **his performance**: better the performance, there will be increase in the compensation.
- Through **his experience:** as the employees devote his years in the organization, expects to get an increased pay for his experience.
- Through **his potential** : the more the potential or talent in the employee the more will be his compensation

EXTERNAL FACTORS: The factors that exist out of the organization but do affect the employee compensation in one or the other way. These factors are as follows:

- **Job Needs:** Jobs Vary greatly in terms of the difficulty, complexity and challenges. Some job needs high level of skills and knowledge while others can be handled by almost everyone,, thus those workers performing complex, challenging task are paid more than the others.

- **Demand & Supply of Labor:** It is one of the important factors affecting wages. The low wage is given, in case, the demand is less and the supply of labor is more. On the other hand, high pay is given, in case, the demand is more and the supply of labor is less.

- **Prevailing Wage Rate:** The compensation is also decided on the basis of the rate that is prevailing in the market, i.e. the amount the other organizations are paying for the same kind of work as the organizations have to pay accordingly to keep the employees with them.

  - **Productivity of worker:** This is the current trend in most of the organization where workers compensation is linked to their productivity levels. The compensation increases with the increase in the production. Therefore, to earn more, the workers need to work on their efficiencies, and need to improve the productivity to get increase in compensation.

  - **Cost of Living:** The cost of living index also influences the employee compensation, in a way, that with the increase or fall in the general price level and the consumer price index, the wage or salary is to be changed accordingly.

  - **Labor Unions:** The powerful and organized labor unions also influence the compensation plan of the company. Higher wages have to be paid by the firm to its workers under the pressure of these trade unions.

  - **Government & Labor laws:** Government has also fixed the rules for protecting the interest of the employees. The organizations are liable to pay as per the government instructions. Wages cannot be fixed below the level prescribed by the government. Beside that there are several laws passed by the Government to protect the workers from the exploitation of employers. The payment of wages Act 1936, The Minimum wages act 1948, The payment of Bonus Act 1965, Equal Remuneration Act 1976, Payment of Gratuity Act 1972 are some of the acts passed in the welfare of the labor, and all the employers must abide by these.

Thus, there are several internal and external factors that decide the amount of compensation to be given to the workers for the amount of work done by them.

Theories of Compensation:

As already defined that the compensation is the remuneration given to the employees for the work they do for the organization ie an employee is entitled to both the monetary and non monetary benefits in return for his contribution to the organization. To understand which component of compensation is efficient, we need to go through the theories of compensation. There are three main theories that are used by Human Resources Department to develop compensation management plans are : also in shown fig 3.3:

1. Reinforcement Theory
2. Equity Theory
3. Agency Theory

- **Reinforcement theory or Reinforcement and Expectancy Theory:** This theory is based on the assumption that, the reward-earning behavior is likely to be repeated, i.e. an employee would do the same thing again for which he was rewarded or acknowledged earlier. It is similar to that of operant conditioning. As also mentioned in Expectancy Theory, given by Vroom, the employee is motivated to do a particular thing for which he is sure or is expected that performance will provide him definite reward or an outcome. The positive reaction motivates one to do the same actions again because one would hope of getting the same or a similar reward.

- **Equity theory:** This theory emphasizes that there should be equity or the uniformity in the pay structure of an employee's remuneration. The productivity of the employees' will be changed if they feel they are not being paid fairly, for the amount of work he does in a day, this will result in lower productivity, increased turnover and high absenteeism. For example, if you and Ram work for the same number of hours and have the same type of job and a similar level of work experience, you would expect to be paid fairly and about the same salary. However, if you find that Ram is paid more than you are, then your productivity will probably decrease so that you are only working up to the level that is fair based on your new assumption of your compensation. The remuneration system should comply with three types of equity

Internal Equity: The employee should perceives that there is the fairness in pay for different jobs based on the nature of work involved,

i.e. he must feel that pay differentials among the jobs are fair.

External Equity: To avoid heavy turnover in hospitality industry, the employee should feel the fairness in what they are being paid is in similar to with what other employers in the same industry are paying to their employees for the same kind of job.

Individual Equity: The employee perceives the pay differentials among the individuals who are performing the same kind of a job and within the same organization. Usually, an individual with more experience gets high remuneration as compared to the fresher irrespective of the nature of a job.

Thus this theory states that the compensation in the form of salary or wages can be decided on the basis of the outcome or the behavior of an employee.

- **Agency theory:** This theory suggests that both the employer and the employee are the stakeholders of the company, and the remuneration paid to the employee is the agency cost. The employee will try to get an increased agency cost whereas the employer will try to minimize it. Therefore, the remuneration should be decided in such a way that the interest of both the parties can be aligned or kept intact.

The three category of people who are closely associated with the organisation are : employee, employer and stakeholder: while employees wants a safe workplace, to be paid fairly based on his level of effort and maybe even have some share in company profits if the firm is successful. As after all, the company could not be able to make profits without employees.

Employer or Management wants to increase the productivity of employees and to be paid fairly based on their level of expertise within the organization. Whereas Stockholders want the company to maximize profits by reducing costs (including labor expenses) while increasing the value and reputation of the company.

As it is clear, that the priorities of each group are in direct conflict. The agency theory of compensation management can make it a priority to maximize productivity, performance and the reputation of the company so that employees, management and stockholders all can ultimately have the same goal.

Compensation Policy:

It includes:

- Compensation policy should be developed after taking into consideration the views of employers, employees, competitors, consumers and the community.
- Compensation policy should be fair, honest and well designed keeping in mind all the factors associated.
- The compensation policy or wage policy should be clearly defined to ensure uniform and consistent application.
- The compensation policy should match with overall plans or goals of the organization.
- Compensation planning should be part and parcel of financial planning
- Management should always inform the wage/salary related policies to their employees.
- Workers should also be included in formulation, drafting and implementation of wage policy
- All wage and salary related decisions should be checked against the standards set in advance in the wage/salary

policy
- To manage compensation related matters adequate information/data should be collected, developed and stored for future planning and execution.
- The compensation policy and programme should be reviewed and revised periodically in accordance with future needs.

Employee Compensation practices in India:

One of the main objectives of economic planning is to raise the standard living of the people. This means that the benefits of planned economic development should be distributed among the different sections of the society.

As already mentioned above the pay structure of a organization depends upon several factors such as labor market conditions, company paying capacity and legal provision etc.

In India employee compensation is classified into two types – base compensation and supplementary compensation. Base compensation refers to monetary payments to employee in the form of wages or salaries. The term wages refers to the remuneration given to the workers doing manual work while the term salaries refers to the compensation or pay given to the managerial, technical and professional staff.

Wages: Meaning:

The Meaning and Definition of Wage: In the lay man language term wages refers to the 'reward' given to the laborers for their services provided by them. Wages are generally paid to blue collared employees mostly on daily, weekly, fortnightly, monthly, per hour or per unit basis. Here services delivered by the laborer include both physical and mental services.

According to **Benham.** "Wages are the amount of money paid under contract by an employer to a worker for services rendered by the employee."

According to **ILO** "Wages refer to that payment which is made by the employers to the laborer for his services hired on the conditions of payment per hour, per day, per week or per fortnight."

While salaries have components, wages unlike salaries do not have a structure or components and they are basically time based ie If a worker is unable to come on the job or remain absent from the work due to illness or goes on a vacation, he loses his wages for

the time he's missed. But on the bright side, these workers are entitled to Overtime Pay, over if the work overtime on holidays/weekends, he will be paid for that.

Wages unlike salaries neither have components for allowances nor for benefits as well. Therefore wages should be so determined that they are perceived to be fair and equitable by all the employees.

<u>Concepts of Wages/types of wages:</u>

If we see from employee's point of view, wages determines his standard of living. Therefore it is an important issue for the developing country like India , and recognizing its importance, the Constitution of India guaranteed _equal pay for equal work' for both men and women'(Article 39). After Independence the Government decided that the wages of the workers cannot be left on the fluctuations of demand and supply of labour so decided to have fix statutory minimum rates and come with this concept of wages.

<u>The concepts of minimum, living and fair wages:</u>

- Minimum Wage
- Fair Wage
- Living Wage

Minimum wage: Minimum wage include that wage which must be compulsorily be paid by the company, whether the company is big or small, making profit or not. It is the bare minimum which a worker can expect to get for services delivered by him.

<u>Objective of minimum wage:</u>

i. To prevent exploitation of workers and ensuring a wage equal to work load.
ii. To raise the value of wages in the company where they are low, thereby removing inequality among industry.
iii. To encourage peace in industry.
iv. iv If there will be guaranteed wage rate this will enable employees to meet their minimum requirements.
v. It help to raise the standards of living and efficiency of workers.

Fair wage: Fair wage is that wage which is above the minimum wage but below the living wage as defined by Marshall and Pigou.

To improve the relationship between labor and management it was asked to pay fair wages to labors, for this Govt. of India appointed a fair wages committee in 1948, clearly defining the fair wages.

According to committee on fair wage 1948 fair wage should be decided after taking into consideration:

1. The productivity of labor
2. The prevailing rate of wages in the same or similar job in the same region or neighboring locality.
3. The place of the industry in the economy.
4. The level of national income and its distribution.
5. The employer's capacity to pay.

Living wage: The living wage is the highest among the three as mentioned by the committee on fair wages, it must provide:

1. Basic amenities of life
2. Efficiency of worker
3. Satisfy social needs of workers such as medical, education, retirement etc

The living wage thus represents higher level of wage; which includes all amenities which a citizen living in a modern society could afford.

State Regulations of Wages:

The Government of India after Independence has adopted different methods to keep a control or regulate wages in India like by prescribing minimum wage rates, regulating payment of wages, settlement of disputes related to wages, setting wage boards etc the step taken by Government of India are:

- **Minimum Wages Act 1948:** In order to prescribe the minimum rate of wages to the employee, the minimum wages act 1948 was passed. The act empowers the government to fix minimum rates for this a tripartite body was formed constituting of employer, unions and government, to advise and assist in fixing and revising the minimum wage rates. The time period or interval for reviewing these minimum wage rates should not exceed more than five years.

- **The Payment of Wages Act, 1936:** The main objective of the act is to provide regular payment of wages without any unauthorized reductions or deductions of wages of the persons who are employed in any industrial establishment or any factory or railway or by a railway contractor whose monthly wage is less than Rs 1600.

The act prescribes the following permissible deductions to be made from the employee's salary:

- Fines or deduction for absence from the job with no valid reason
- Deduction for (i) loss of goods entrusted to worker
- House given by employer
- Services provided by employer
- advances given to worker
- tax payable by employer
- Deduction under court orders, cooperative society.
- Provident fund, insurance premium, etc.

Wage board: It is one of the important boards set up by the Government of India for fixation and revision of wages. Government of India started the set up of wage boards on the basis of recommendations made during Second Five year Plan, which were reiterated by the Third Five- year Plan. Wage Boards are appointed on an ad- hoc basis by the Government as they are not governed by any legislation.

Each Wage Boards consists of one neutral Chairman, two independent members and two or three representative of workers and management each. The responsibility of the formed Wage Board is to study various factors related to wages, before making any recommendations. The recommendations of Wage Boards are first send to the Government for acceptance. The Government may accept with or without modification or reject the recommendations of the Wage Board. The recommendations if accepted by the Government are enforceable by the parties concerned.

The Wage Boards takes following factors into consideration for fixing or revising the wages in various industries:

1. Job evaluation
2. Wages rates for similar jobs in comparable industries
3. Employees productivity
4. Firms' ability to pay
5. Various wage legislations
6. Existing level of wage differentials and their desirability
7. Governments objectives regarding social justice, social equality, economic justice and economic equality
8. Place of the industry in the economy and the society of the country and the region
9. Need for incentive, improvement in productivity etc.

The Wage Boards fix and revise various components of wages like basic pay, dearness allowance, incentive earnings, overtime pay, house rent allowance and all other allowances.

- **Compulsory Conciliation and Arbitration:** With the objective of providing the environment of conciliation and arbitration, the industrial Disputes Act 1947 was passed. It provides for the appointment of Industrial Tribunals and National Industrial Tribunals for settlement of industrial disputes including those relating to wages. The main aim of this act was to settle the dispute.

- **Workmen's Compensation Act, 1923:** The Workmen's Compensation Act of 1923, also called as employee's compensation act in today's world was a turning point in the history of labour jurisprudence and trade union movement. This legislation provided for the first time, compensation to the workman from their employers for the injury which employee suffered from the result of an accident during the course of employment

This principal initiated that a workman, who suffers injury or get injured within the course of his employment, should be entitled to compensation and in case of fatal injury his dependents should be compensated. By this Act a mental and emotional security was provided to the workman whose disability otherwise would have resulted in a loss in the earning capacity.

SUMMARY:

Every action human takes is due to some inner drive which force him to take necessary steps to satisfy those needs, this inner force is called motivation. In organisation, employee motivation refers to the enthusiasm, energy level, commitment and the amount of creativity that an employee brings to the organization on a daily basis. Motivated employees act as an asset to an organization, as motivation is directly proportional to an organization's success. As each employee is different from other employee, his source of motivation may be different to others so HR should plan accordingly and apply the right type of motivation to increase the level of employee satisfaction and commitment. Here some employees respond better to intrinsic motivation- ie they respond more towards their inner dive. While others may respond better to extrinsic motivations which respond more towards rewards and recognition.

Some theories to explain motivation are: Maslow's hierarchy of need – Maslow explained that each individual works to satisfy the inner drives which are formed into pyramidal shape of hierarchy of needs He further suggested that individual will move to next source or need only when his initial need is satisfied. Another most explained theory is of Herzberg two factor theory- motivational factors and Hygiene Factors. The motivational factors if present will automatically raise the morale of the employee. While if Hygiene factors are absent this will de-motivate the employee but if present it will not de-motivate the employee but will not motivate also.

Another theory is Reinforcement Theory: which suggest employee will repeat his behavior if his behavior has got reward in the past so this will motivate employee to repeat those action which they knew will be rewarded. Then there was Equity Theory which suggested that Individuals not only are concern with what they receive in return of their services but compare their job inputs and outcomes with those of others and then respond so as to remove any kind of inequalities. Motivational factors can be divided into two-Monetary and nonmonetary factors.

Compensation is what employee receives in exchange for their contribution to the organization. Generally employee provides their services to receive three types of rewards – pays refers to the base wages and salaries which the employee receive in return, for the work done by them. Second includes -Compensation in the form of incentives which includes bonuses, commission and profit sharing plans are specially designed by the organization to motivate and encourage the employee to perform beyond expectations. Thirdly- the benefits like insurance, medical and educational, and retirement facilities etc are indirect type of compensation offered by the organization, keeping in mind the goodwill and benefit of employee. Thus compensation is a comprehensive term including all pay, incentives and benefits offered by employees for the services they perform in the organization.

In India after independence regulatory bodies and act were formulated to safeguard the interest of the employee and daily laborers. Salaries are given to employee and Wages are given to the daily laborers for the services provided by them three types of wages - Minimum wages, fair wages and living wages.

Wage Board was formed to take care of the interest of the employee and laborer. Act to settle the dispute and tribunals were formed to take care of the interest of the employee.

Keywords:

Motivation: Motivation refers to the process by which human needs direct and control the behavior of a human being.

Motives: Motives are the primary energizers of behavior which prompt people to action.

Motivators: Motivators are associated with positive feelings of employees about the job.

Intrinsic Motivation: It refers to incentives internal to the job and provides satisfaction during the performance of work itself.

Extrinsic Motivation : refers to the incentives which are external to the job, such as, alary, fringe benefits, etc.

Job Enrichment : It refers to the process whereby a job is enriched in terms of its contents, responsibility, scope, variety and challenge.

Goals: Goals are the ends which provide satisfaction of human needs.

Self actualization :It refers to realizing one's potentiality for continued self-development and for being creative in the broadest sense of the word.

Compensation : it is what employees receive in exchange for their contribution to the organization.

Incentives : Motivations devices used to encourage special work effort such as bonuses or commissions.

Wages: The amount paid by the employees for the services of hourly, daily, weekly fortnightly employees. (ILO)

Salaries : Remuneration paid to the clerical and management personal employed on a monthly or yearly basis. However the distinction between wages and salaries need not be observed in actual wages. Both may mean remuneration paid to an employee for services rendered.

Earnings : Total amount of remuneration received by an employee during a given period.

Wage Policy: Principles acting as guidelines for determining a wage structure.

Minimum Wage : wage sufficient to sustain and preserve the efficiency of the worker and to provide him basic amenities.

Wage Structure : Consists of various pay scale showing ranges of pay within each grade.

FOUR

JOB SATISFACTION, ORGANISATIONAL CULTURE, DISCIPLINARY ACTION

<u>INTRODUCTION:</u>

In this unit previously we have learnt about motivation which throws light on the actual behavior of employees on their jobs. Job satisfaction on the other hand, is concerned with their feeling and attitudes towards their jobs throwing light on their potential behavior. In the words of Feldman & Arnold —Job satisfaction is the amount of overall positive effect or feelings that individual have towards their jobs.

—Job satisfaction is the amount of pleasure or contentment associated with the job. If you like your job intensity that you will experience high Job satisfaction while if you dislike your job intensity, than you will experience Job dissatisfaction‖. Job satisfaction is an individual's emotional reaction to the job itself. It is his attitude towards his job.

The other part of unit deals with organizational culture which has great impact on organization morale and motivation as it is this organizational culture which distinguishes one organization from other it is similar to the personality of individual which is unique in the same way organizational culture or its organization value, believes, norms etc are unique.

It is essential to maintain discipline in the organization. Discipline means an orderly behavior in the organization where all employees follow the rules, regulations and instructions laid down by the management in the organization. It also suggest what action to be taken if any misconduct or indiscipline takes place in the organization.

Human Resource Management is basically a process of dealing with people. A manager especially HR manger has to deal with various types of employee who may also be temperamental, emotionally weak or strong, the instrument with which manager develop and maintain a congenial interpersonal relationship with employee is Counseling. Counseling tries to improve the mental health of the employee and helps to overcome employee grievances and maintains discipline in the organization.

JOB SATISFACTION - DEFINITION:

E. A. Locke describe job satisfaction as, —the pleasurable emotional state resulting from the appraisal of one's job as achieving or facilitating the achievement of one's job values‖ According to P. E. Spector, —Job satisfaction is the extent to which people like or dislike their jobs‖.

De Nobile defined job satisfaction as —the extent to which a staff member has favorable or positive feelings about work or the work environment.‖

Ivancevich et al. defined job satisfaction as —the feeling and perception of a worker regarding his/her work and how he or she feels well in an organization‖.

Davis, Newstrom, and Dessler describe job satisfaction as —a set of favorable or unfavorable feelings for the employees to perceive their work and that determine the possibility of a major disposition to achieve higher performance‖.

According to S.P. Robbins, —Job satisfaction refers to an individual's general attitude toward his or her job.

Thus in short we can say that the Job Satisfaction is the extent to which people like or are satisfied or dislike or dissatisfied with their jobs. This could be the job in general or other aspects of the job like: their colleagues, pay or working conditions. In addition to that, the extent to which work outcomes meet or exceed expectations may determine the level of job satisfaction.

Importance of Job Satisfaction:

Job satisfaction has been linked to many variables, including productivity, absenteeism, turnover, etc. It is significant because a person's attitude and beliefs may affect his or her behavior.

Importance of job satisfaction are-:

Lower Turnover: High Labor Turnover is one of the biggest lacuna for any organization and it is the well known fact that a person is more likely to be actively searching for another job if they have low satisfaction; whereas, a person who is satisfied with their job is less likely to be job seeking. It has been found that Job satisfaction is inversely co- related to turnover ie satisfied employees less turn over vice versa.

Higher Productivity: Irrespective of job title and pay grade, employees who have high job satisfaction results in achieving higher productivity. When someone is happy with their job, they focus well and they pay attention to their tasks. They seem themselves responsible and accountable for achieving the organizational goal that does make them happy. When one member of a team displays high productivity, it is natural for other members of the team to try to increase productivity at the desired level.

Increased Customer Satisfaction: It is a well known fact that if employees feel safe and satisfied in the organization, it can lead to higher sales, lower costs and a stronger bottom line. Basically, profit can be earned by selling, the products or giving services to the customers. If the employees are satisfied with their job then they can give better customer service and we know that customer retention and loyalty are dependent on the basis of the given service of the employees. If customer's loyalty is increased, automatically it will lead to not only to increase profit but also increase goodwill in the society for the organization.

Employee Absenteeism: A employee satisfied from his job will understand his responsibility and likely to attend the job even if they have minor problems like cold etc, whereas an unsatisfied employee will be more likely to remain absent from the work, calling them sick even when they are well enough, i.e. taking mental health rest off not due to illness or personal reason but just to avoid work or skipping from responsibility.

Helps to earn higher revenues: Even the training or motivation can't help, until and unless an individual develops a feeling of attachment and loyalty for his organization. Most of the employee's waste half of their time fighting with their peers or sorting out issues, frustrating about their conditions. While a satisfied employee is the happy employee who willingly helps their fellow worker and cooperate with each other in the organization even during emergency situations. For them, their organization comes first, they believe that the organizational goals and objectives are their own goals and objectives, and they really feel for the organization. They take pride in representing their respective organization and work hard to ensure higher revenues for the organization.

Satisfied Employees tend to handle pressure: Satisfied employees accept challenges with a big smile and deliver even in the worst of circumstances. Employees who are happy with their jobs are willing to participate in training programs and are eager to learn new technologies, software which would eventually help them in their professional career. Satisfied employees are the ones who are extremely loyal towards their organization and stick to it even in the worst scenario. They do not work out of any compulsion but because they dream of taking their organization to a new level. Employees need to be passionate towards their work and passion comes only when employees are satisfied with their job and organization on the whole.

Factors affecting the level of job satisfaction are:

1. Working Environment.
2. Fair Policies and Practice.
3. Caring Organization.
4. Appreciation.
5. Pay.
6. Age.
7. Promotion.
8. Feel of Belongings.
9. Initiation and Leadership.
10. Feel of Being Loved.
11. Safety and Security.
12. Challenges.
13. Responsibilities.
14. Creativity in Job.
15. Personal Interest and Hobbies.
16. Respect from Co-Workers.
17. Relationship with Supervisors.
18. Feedback.
19. Flexibility.
20. Nature of Work.

Theory of Job Satisfaction & Motivation:

Satisfaction is a psychological factor. We cannot see it nor can we measure it, but their expressions in the human mind can be easily identified. When an employee is satisfied with his assigned task and can discharge his responsibility satisfactorily, it is called job satisfaction. Job satisfaction theories have a strong overlap with theories explaining human motivation.

The most common and prominent job satisfaction theories are;

1. Maslow's Needs Hierarchy Theory
2. Herzberg's Motivator-Hygiene Theory
3. Job Characteristics Model
4. Dispositional Approach

Hierarchy of needs: Maslow needs hierarchy theory is commonly known for explaining the motivation and needs of the human. Maslow's needs hierarchy theory was one of the first theories to examine the important contributors to job satisfaction. The theory suggested that there is five level hierarchy or pyramid which forms the human needs they are: physiological needs, safety, belongingness or love, esteem, and self-actualization. Maslow further suggested that once the basic or essentials need of human are met (such as, physiological needs and safety), than only he proceed further for more complex needs (such as, belonging and esteem).

Maslow's need theory was developed to explain human motivation in general. Though this theory if applied in work area can easily be correlated with job satisfaction also.

In the organization, some of the basic or physiological needs which an employee desire for is good pay, canteen etc and for safety needs he desire for that he is physically safe in their work environment, as well as job security and suitable company structures and policies. When these needs of him are satisfied, than only he can focus on feeling of belongingness which comes from healthy and positive relationships with colleagues and supervisors in the workplace, Once satisfied, than the employee will look for esteem, to feel as though they are valued and appreciated by their colleagues and their organization thereby meeting the belonging and esteem need. The final step is where the employee seeks to self-actualize where they need to grow and develops in order to become everything what they are capable of becoming.

Therefore, if organizations trying to improve employee job satisfaction should first attempt to meet the basic needs of employees before progressing to meet the higher-order needs. However, now days this theory is becoming obsolete as it does not consider the cognitive process of the employee and, in general, lacks empirical supporting evidence. Beside that there has been difficulty in measuring what the final goal is or when it has been achieved.

Motivator-Hygiene Theory: Herzberg's motivator-hygiene theory suggests that job satisfaction and dissatisfaction are two opposite factors which are not related to each other. As _Motivating' factors for employees in the organization are like pay and benefits, recognition and achievement need to be met in order for an employee to be satisfied with work. On the other hand, hygiene factors such as, working conditions, company policies and structure, job security, interactions with colleagues and quality of management are associated with job dissatisfaction.

As both the hygiene and motivational factors are independent factors as mentioned above. This theory suggest that when hygiene factors are less the employee is dissatisfied, but when these factors are high it means the employee is not dissatisfied (or neutral), but not necessarily satisfied. As employee's satisfaction is dependent on the motivator factors. As believed, when motivators are met the employee is thought to be satisfied. There might be complexity, that he might feel both satisfied and dissatisfied at the same time; or neither satisfied nor dissatisfied. This becomes its drawback as Motivator-Hygiene theory was not able to distinguish the job from satisfaction and dissatisfaction; the theory itself has received little empirical support.

Job Characteristics Model: This Job Characteristics Model (JCM) suggests that job satisfaction occurs when the organization work environment encourages intrinsically motivating characteristics like job characteristics: skill variety, task identity, task significance, autonomy and feedback, these five job characteristics will influence three psychological states as shown in figure. These three psychosocial states will then lead to a number of potential outcomes, which also includes: job satisfaction. Thus if we see from the point of view of an organization, it is believed that by improving the five core job dimensions this will finally lead to a better work environment and increased job satisfaction.

Dispositional Approach: This dispositional approach believes that job satisfaction is highly related to personality. It suggests that an individual has a strong inclination towards a certain level of satisfaction, and that these remain quiet stable even with the passage of time. The evidence can be seen through indirect studies and direct studies.

Most prominently, the research evidence that shows - self-esteem, self-efficacy, emotional stability and locus of control comprise a major part of our personality, which contribute to how an individual sees himself. A review of 169 correlations, between each of four affective constructs (i.e., self-esteem, self-efficacy, emotional stability and locus of control) and job satisfaction, found that as these four affective increases so as job satisfaction also increases.

Summary Of Theories: Thus in the end it can be seen that despite being most popular - hierarchy of needs and motivator-hygiene approaches but there is little empirical support for these two theories in terms of job satisfaction while on the other hand, the dispositional approach and JCM have gain huge empirical support. Though, it can also not be denied that motivating factors has great influence on the surrounding work environment which ultimately has an impact on how satisfied employees are at their work, and the personality or the JCM do not fully explain job satisfaction. Therefore, Furnham and colleagues integrated Herzberg's motivator-hygiene approach and personality traits to check the combined impact of them on job satisfaction. Finally revealing that demographic variables and scores on the five commonly used personality traits (including, openness, conscientiousness, extraversion, agreeableness, and neuroticism) together had a significant impact on job satisfaction

Correlates of Job Satisfaction/ Determinants of Job Satisfaction:

Several studies have been carried out in the past to identify the correlates of high and low job satisfaction. These studies have related the job satisfaction to two types of variables which are organizational variables and personal variables:-

Organizational variables: it includes

1. **Occupational level**: Higher the level of the job, the greater or more will be the satisfaction of the individual. This happens because higher level jobs carry great prestige and self control. This relationship has come from social reference group theory where the society values some jobs as compared to others ie people in valued jobs will like it more than those who are in non valued jobs.

2. **Job Content**: - The more variations in job content with less repetitiveness in how the task to be performed it will leads to greater job satisfaction of the individual.

3. **Considerate Leadership**: - everyone likes to be treated with care and considerations, ie considerate leadership will results in higher job satisfaction than with inconsiderate leader

4. **Pay & Promotional Opportunities**: -If all other things being equal these two variables are positively related, i.e. higher the pay or promotional opportunities the more will be the job satisfaction.

5. **Interaction in the work group**: - Job satisfaction generally increases when an individual is accepted at his work place, by his peers, he has high need of affiliation.

Personal variables: It includes

1. **Age**: - Most of the evidences have shown that there exist a positive relation between age and the Job Satisfaction up to the preretirement years, as workers in their advance age have adjusted with their job condition.

2. **Educational Level**:- If the occupational level remain constant than it is seen that there is negative relationship between job satisfaction and educational level as higher the education higher is the individual expectations to evaluate his job rewards on the basis of his education level.

3. **Sex:** - There are no constant evidence that women are more satisfied with their jobs than men keeping factors like job and occupational level constant. This might be believed it is due to lower occupational aspiration of women.

4. **Experience**: - Job satisfaction tends to increase with increasing years of experience. But it may decrease after 20 years when employee do not understand their job expectations

Measuring Job Satisfaction:

The commonly used methods to measure job satisfaction of the employees are:-

1. Single Global Rating.
2. Summation Score.

- Job Diagnostic Survey.
- Job Satisfaction Index.
- Job Satisfaction Survey.
- Minnesota Satisfaction Questionnaire.
- Job Satisfaction Relative to Expectations.
- Global Job Satisfaction.

- Job Descriptive Index (JDI).

1. **Single Global Rating:** In this method employees are asked direct questions like —how satisfied are you with your job‖

2. **Summation Score:** This method identifies the key elements of the job and ask the employees to respond how they feel about each element, these elements include nature of the work, supervision, present pay, promotion opportunities, and relation with co-workers. There are different ways of measuring job satisfaction are:-

a. **Job Descriptive Index (JDI)**

This method was developed by Smith, Kendall, and Hulin in 1969. In this there are 72 items in the index which assess five facets of job satisfaction which includes: the work, pay, promotions, supervision, and coworkers. With the help of combination of ratings of satisfaction a composite measure of job satisfaction is determined.

b. **Global Job Satisfaction**

This method was developed during 1979, by Cook, and Wall which includes 15 items to decide the overall job satisfaction. In this two subscales were prepared taking into account extrinsic and intrinsic aspects of the job, out of which the extrinsic has eight items and the intrinsic has seven items.

c. **Job Satisfaction Relative to Expectations**

This method was developed by Bacharach, Bamberger, and Conley. It measures the degree of agreement between the perceived quality of broad aspects of a job and employee expectations.

d. **Minnesota Satisfaction Questionnaire**

This a questionnaire having 100 questions based on 20 subscales which measure satisfaction with ability, utilization, achievement, activity, advancement, authority, company policies and practices, compensation, co-workers, creativity, independence, moral values, recognition, responsibility, security, social service, social status, supervision- human relations, supervision-technical variety, and working conditions.

e. **Job Satisfaction Survey**

This method was developed by Spector, having 36 items based on nine job facets. The job facets include pay, promotion, supervision, benefits; contingent rewards Operating procedures, co-workers, nature of work and communication.

f. **Job Satisfaction Index**

This method was developed by Schriescheim and Tsue, having six items which becomes the index to determine overall job satisfaction. The items are the work, supervision, co- workers, pay, promotion opportunities, and the job in general.

g. **Job Diagnostic Survey**

This method of survey was developed by Hackman and Oldham which measures both overall and specific facets of job satisfaction. It has three dimensions of overall job satisfaction which includes general satisfaction, internal work motivation, and growth satisfaction, which are combined into a single measure. The facets which are measured on the survey include security, compensation, co-workers, and supervision.

ORGANISATION CULTURE-INTRODUCTION:

An organizational culture is present in all organizations, and has huge impact on the morale and motivation of organizational members. Just like every human has a unique personality which describe him the best and separate him from others, Organizational culture does the same for the organization, every company has its own unique personality similar to that of a unique personality of an individual. This unique personality of an organization is termed as its culture. In groups of people who work together for the organization, organizational culture is an invisible but powerful force that influences the behavior of the members of that group.

The general definition of organizational culture as stated by Martins and Martins (2003, p 380) is —a system of shared meaning held by members, distinguishing the organization from other organizations. Arnold (2005, p 625) indicates that —organizational culture is the distinctive norms, beliefs, principles and ways of behaving that combine to give each organization its distinct character‖.

These two definitions clearly suggest that main role of organizational culture is to distinguish one organization from another organization i.e. just like personality differentiates one individual from others similarly organizational culture differentiates one organization from other. It is that distinguishing feature used for separating organization from one another.

In link with the above definitions, Schein (1985, p 9) also defines organizational culture as

—a pattern of basic assumptions invented, discovered, or developed by a given group as it learns to cope with its problems of external adaptation and internal integration that has worked well enough to be considered valid, and therefore, to be taught to new members as the correct way to perceive, think, and feel in relation to those problems‖.

Thus organizational culture is a system of shared assumptions, values, and beliefs, which controls how people behave in the organizations. These shared values have a strong influence on the people in the organization which decides how employees will act, and perform their jobs. Every organization develops and maintains a unique culture, which provides guidelines and boundaries for the behavior of the members of the organization.

Methods of Observing and Learning organizational culture:

Organizational culture is a pattern of basic assumptions that are considered valid and that are taught and learnt by the new members as the way to perceive, think, and feel in the organization. Brown (1998, p 10 – 30) suggested the following ways have been identified to be methods observation and learning the organization's culture:

- Artifacts: This refers to symbols of culture in the physical and socially constructed environment of an organization is called **artifacts.** Artifacts are the most visible and accessible level of culture. Examples of artifacts include office space, equipments, rules, systems and procedures.

- Personal Enactment: Personal enactment is behavior that reflects the organization's values.

- Language. It refers to the fundamental way in which the organization comprehends its world. Examples of language include jokes, metaphors, stories, myths and legends.

- Behavior patterns. : They refer to relatively elaborate sets of behavior which are the features of organizational life that are enacted repeatedly on important occasions. These patterns include rites, rituals, ceremonies and celebrations.

- Ceremonies and Rites: Ceremonies can be divided into organizational rites, including rites of passage, rites of enhancement, rites of renewal, rites of integration, rites of conflict reduction, and rites of degradation. They are relatively elaborate sets of activities.

- Rituals: The practices which are repeated frequently are known as rituals.

- Norms of Behavior. They refer to the rules for the behavior which describe what is considered to be appropriate and inappropriate responses from employees in certain circumstances. Such norms develop after a period of time as individuals discuss and negotiate with each other to reach a consensus or midway on how to deal with organizational issues.

- Stories: Stories are the rich source of carriers of organizational culture that give meaning and identity to organizations and help in orienting the new employees. There are stories about the boss, stories about getting fired, stories about how the company deals with employees who have to relocate, stories about whether lower- level employees can rise to the top, stories about how the company deals with crisis situations, and stories about how status considerations work when rules are broken.
- Heroes. These provide role models and portray the organization to external constituencies. Heroes are the people who motivate other employees. This helps in making success possible.
- Symbols and symbolic action. Symbols communicate the culture through unspoken messages and include words, objects, conditions, acts or characteristics of the organization, which mean something to organizational members. Typical symbols found in organizations are corporate logos, policies and products and even mental images held by employees.

Functions of Organisational Culture:

The main function of organizational culture is to define the way of doing things in order to give meaning to organizational life (Arnold, 2005) Organizational culture also determines organizational behavior, by identifying principal goals; work methods; how members should interact and address each other; and how to conduct personal relationships (Harrison, 1993).

Brown (1998, p 89- 91) states the following functions of organizational culture:

Reduction in Conflict: A common culture helps in promoting consistency of perception, problem definition, evaluation of issues and opinions, and preferences for action.

Coordination and control: As organizational culture promotes consistency in outlook thereby it facilitates effective co-ordination and control in the organizational processes .

Reduction of uncertainty: When organization accepts the cultural mind frame it helps as an anxiety reducing device which simplifies the world of work, makes choices easier and rational action seem possible.

Motivation: An appropriate and cohesive culture can provide employees a focus of identification and loyalty, and inculcate beliefs and values that encourage employees to perform.

Competitive advantage: Strong culture increases the chances of the organization's to be successful in the marketplace.

In addition to the above functions, Martins and Martins (2003, p 382) also mention the following as functions of organizational culture:

- It helps in defining the boundary i.e. a boundary-defining role, which means, it helps in creating distinctions between one organization and the other organizations.
- It gives a sense of identity to organizational members.

- It encourages commitment within the employees towards the organization which is something larger than individual self-interests.
- It improves social system stability which acts as the social glue that helps to bind the organization by giving proper standards for what employees should say and do.
- It acts as a meaningful control mechanism that guides or shapes the attitudes and behaviors of employees.

Organisational Culture Model:

There are various descriptive models that try to identify different types of organizational culture in the field of organizational development. Harrison (1993) presents a theoretical model for the purpose of diagnosing organizational culture:

Harrison (1993, p 8) states that —though the model is intended to be descriptive rather than evaluative; there is a tendency to perceive it in evaluative terms‖. This descriptive model helps to identify the culture, and gap between the existing and preferred cultures in an organization (Harrison, 1993). This model states that organizational culture can be diagnosed in four cultural dimensions, namely power-oriented culture; role- oriented culture; achievement-oriented culture; and support-oriented culture (Harrison, 1993).

Power culture dimension: In an organization with a power culture, much importance is given to use of power in order to exercise control and influence behavior Brown (1998, p 66) suggest that —a power culture has a single source of power from which rays of influence spread throughout the organization. This means that here power is centralized and organizational members or employees are connected to the centre by functional and specialist strings (Harrison, 1993). Figure 2.1 of the organizational culture model indicates that a power-oriented culture organization is characterized by high centralization and low formalization modes of operation.

This type of culture is rule oriented in nature, focusing on respect of authority, rationality in procedures, division of work and normalization (Hampden-Turner, 1990).Where the formal authority or the head is in the centre and holds the power to control and influence activities within the organization, i.e. with those having power will decide what happen in the organization and employees are generally judged by what they achieve rather than how they do things or how they act. A best result of this culture can be quick decision-making, (as no long chains require, decision by those having power) even if those decisions are not in the interest of the organization in the long run.

Role culture dimension: In this type of culture, focus is mainly on job description and specialization. In other words, work is controlled by procedures and rules that explain the job description, for the job. The role-oriented culture as being high in both formalization and centralization on modes of operation.

Brown (1998, p 67) states that —the strength of a role culture lies in its functions or specialties (finance, purchasing, production and so forth) which can be thought of as a series of pillars which are coordinated and controlled by a small group of senior executives‖. This suggests that the working and functions of such an organization are formalized and centralized; which are controlled by role and communication procedures (Hampden-Turner, 1990). Thus organizations with a role culture are based on rules, which are highly controlled, with everyone in the organization knowing what their roles and responsibilities are. Power in a role culture is determined by a person's position (role) in the organizational structure.

Role cultures are built on detailed organizational structures with huge chain of command or hierarchy which also becomes its drawback as decision making becomes a lengthy and slow process and organization has a fear in taking risk. Thus such organizations are often stereotyped and bureaucratic because of its mechanistic procedures.

Achievement culture dimension: Achievement culture is often referred to as task culture, which suggests that organizational members focus on realizing the set purpose and goals of the organization. Brown (1998, p 67) states that —a task culture is one in which power is somewhat diffuse, being based on expertise rather that position or charismal. Task culture forms when teams in an organization are made to deal with specific problems or progress

projects. The task is the important thing, so power within the team will often shift depending on the mix of the team members and the status of the problem or project. To ensure that the task culture proves effective, it will largely be decided on the team dynamic ie with the right mix of skills, personalities and leadership, working in teams can be incredibly productive and creative. That achievement-oriented culture's mode of operation is high in formalization and low in centralization.

Support culture: Support-oriented culture differs from the achievement-oriented culture which believes on teams, and promotes individuals as the central point in the organization. Harrison and Stokes (1992, p 20) define support-oriented culture as an — organizational climate that is based on mutual trust between the individual and the organization‖. Thus, support-oriented organizational culture is often referred to as a person-oriented culture. In organizations which are following these cultures, individuals are given due weight age and they see themselves as unique and superior to the organization. The organization simply exists for the people to work. An organisation with a person culture is really just a collection of individuals who happen to be working for the same organisation.

The organizational structure is a benevolent cluster structure with very less hierarchy, which means less power control of employees (Harrison, 1993). Authority is decided on the basis of task competence; which is very much similar to the role-oriented culture organization. Power sharing and the influence of power can only be applied where there is a need for expert or task competence (Brown, 1998). As a result individuals influence each other through example and helpfulness.

Strong and Weak Organisational Cultures:

Organizational culture can either be weak or strong. Martins and Martins (2003, p 382) suggested that ―in a strong culture, the organization's main or core values are strongly held and shared widely among all‖. This means that when organizational members accept the strong culture having strong shared values, they become more committed towards the organization. Strong organizational culture thus refers to organizations where beliefs and values are shared relatively consistently throughout an organization (Deal & Kennedy, 1982).

Strong organizational cultures also have a great influence on the behavior of organizational members (Martins & Martins, 2003). In other words, a strong culture is a powerful lever for guiding behavior (Deal & Kennedy, 1982) for the employee.

A strong organization culture even helps to achieve high performance as strong culture helps in alignment of goal i.e. employee keep aside their individual goals and work together towards achieving common organization goal and helps in enhancing employee motivation.

One more benefit of strong organizational culture, is that it helps in reducing employee turnover from the organization. This is due to when organizational members agree about what the organization stands for, the end results are cohesiveness, loyalty and organizational commitment (Martins & Martins, 2003).

A weak culture, on the other hand, means the opposite of a strong culture, in other words, organizational members do not subscribe to the shared beliefs, values and norms (O'Reilly et al, 1991). Organizational members in a weak culture find it difficult to identify with the organization's core values and goals (Wilson, 1992). As a result components or different departments within such an organization uphold different beliefs that do not necessarily address the core goals of the organization.

Weak cultures have a negative impact on employees because they are directly linked to increased turnover (Harrison, 1993). In essence, the fundamental strength of the organization's culture is determined by how weak or strong it is.

Importance of Organizational Culture:

Schein (1992) suggests that organizational culture is very much important today than it was earlier because of increased competition, globalization, mergers, acquisitions, alliances, and various workforce developments have created a greater need for the systematic organization culture as it has following characteristics:

Innovation and risk taking: It refers to the extent to which employees are encouraged to be innovative and risk taking. The organization culture promotes innovation at all stages which include:

- Product innovation
- Strategy innovation
- Process innovation and the ability to successfully introduce new technologies, such as Information Technology
- It encourages coordination and integration across organizational units in order to improve efficiency, quality, and speed of designing, manufacturing, and delivering products and services
- It helps in effective management of the dispersed work units and increasing workforce diversity

Organization culture gives attention to details; which refers to the extent to which employees are expected to exhibit precision analysis and attention to details

Organization culture is outcome oriented: It refers to the extent to which focuses is on result rather than on the techniques and processes used to achieve those results.

People orientation: It refers to the extent to which management decision which is taken into consideration, affects the people within organization.

Organization culture believes in team orientation: It refers to the extent to which work activities are organized through teams instead by individuals. Organization culture Facilitate and support teamwork

Aggressive: It refers to the extent to which organization culture suggests that people are aggressive and competitive rather than easy going.

Stabilities: It indicates the extent to which organizational activities emphasis maintaining the status in contrast to growth.

Creating and Sustaining/Maintaining Organizational Culture:

The following topic explains how organization creates and sustains organization culture:

Creating organizational culture: The main source of creating organizational culture is from the organization's leadership. Leadership here refers to all the influential individuals, or founders of the organization who have a major impact on the creation of the organization's early culture (Schein, 1985), who tend to impose their beliefs and values about the nature of the world, organizations and human nature on their organization.‖ Thus organizational culture is not created accidentally or spontaneously but it is through founders who have specific values and beliefs in their endeavor to impart their vision and goals in the organization.

Sustaining organizational culture: In order to keep the organizational culture alive, the organization has to ensure that its culture is transmitted to organizational members (Martins & Martins, 2003).

Brown (1998, p 55 – 59) presents the following three basic stages in which organizational culture can be sustained in the organization:

Pre-selection & Selection: The first stage of managing or sustaining organizational culture is the pre-selection stage. The man goal of this stage is to identify potential recruits who aspire to become members of an organization, who may make great efforts to learn about its history and culture and hire individuals who have the knowledge, skills, and abilities to perform the jobs within the organization successfully

Socialisation: The next stage is the stage of socialisation which is also describe as the —enculturation process by which participants learn the culturally accepted beliefs, values and behaviors, so that they are able to act as effective members of the groupl. As it observed that new employees are not familiar with the organization's culture, thus the organizations want to help their new employees to learn and adapt to its culture and this process that adapts employees to the organization's culture is known as *socialization* (Allen and Meyer). This suggests that during the socialisation stage, the organisation helps new organisational members to adapt to its culture (Martins & Martins, 2003).

Martins and Martins (2003, p 388) conceptualize the socialisation process as consisting of the following three stages:

- The pre-arrival stage – It is the period of learning in the socialization process which occurs before a new employee joins the organization.

- The encounter stage – In this stage the new member sees what the organization is really like and confronts the possibility that expectations and reality may diverge.
- The metamorphosis stage - In this stage a new employee adjusts to his or her work group's values and norms.

Incorporation/Rejection: The incorporation or rejection stage is the final stage of sustaining organizational culture. Through this socialisation process it is decided, that organizational members may be incorporated or rejected (Brown, 1998). The things which Indicates that the individual member has reached full incorporation includes acceptance by the work group, understanding and acceptance of the organization's culture (Martins & Martins, 2003). On the other hand rejection may lead to loss of key goals, values and assumptions; which ultimately create a crisis of identity for organizational members (Schein, 1985).

Changing Organisational Culture:

Organizations should regularly and systematically reassess their cultures, as many environmental changes takes place due to globalization, workforce diversity, and advances in technology. There are different theoretical views on changing or managing organizational culture, which tells that the process of culture change is very complex. O'Reilly (1989) suggested that it is possible to change or manage organizational culture by choosing the attitudes and behaviors that are required, identifying the norms that promote or impede them, and then taking action to create the desired effect.

In relation to that, Arnold (2005, p 579) states that —culture can be seen as something that can be managed or changed when the existing culture is inappropriate or is not suitable enough to meet the organization's competitive needs‖. Therefore, organizations decide to undertake conscious culture change as it becomes necessary to do so (Harrison, 1993).

On the other hand, Martins and Martins (2003, p 395) states that —changing an organization's culture is highly difficult but cultures can be changed‖. Thus, Harrison (1993, p 21) suggested that though it is possible to change the organization culture but it has its own drawbacks also which are:-

- It is very much difficult to get the deep changes in values and management style and in organization systems, structures, and rewards systems.
- Changing the organization is a time consuming process as it takes a long time, three to five years or much more.
- It creates huge turmoil and stress within the organization as it become unclear to what to do.
- It affects the productivity of the employees, than the leadership and finally the goodwill of market also gets affected thus making it more difficult to change and manage.

Brown (1998, p 189 – 192) suggested the following steps, which can be followed during the process of managing organizational culture change:

Step 1: Analyzing the existing culture – first identify the existing culture; identify the latest trends of the market than try to establishing a norm gap that exist between your culture and the market.

Step 2: Experiencing the desired culture – check the others systems, judge which is best suitable for your organization, introduce it and get involved in it.

Step 3: Modifying the existing culture –Once you identify the most suitable culture for your organization, install the system in your organization.

Step 4: Sustaining the desired culture –Once installed new culture should be periodically and systematically evaluated and renewal.

In essence, changing the organization's culture is possible, but attempts to initiate such a process should take into consideration the complexity of culture.

DISCIPLINE:

Discipline means orderly behavior- suggesting a voluntary and willing compliance of rules, regulations, and instructions as well as development of right habits of conducting work with others at the work-place. Discipline involves regulation and modulation of human activities to produce a controlled performance in the organization. It is the orderly conduct of affairs by the members of an organization who follows and abides by its necessary regulations because they desire to cooperate harmoniously and wants healthy and peaceful work environment for all.

Discipline main aim is to encourage employees to confirm to establish standards of job performance and to behave sensibly and safely at work place. According to Richard D. Calhoon, —Discipline is the force that prompts individuals or groups to observe rules, regulations, standards and procedures deemed necessary for an

Organizationl. Therefore discipline means securing consistent behavior in accordance with the accepted norms of behavior. Thus the main objective of discipline is to gain willing acceptance of the rules, regulations, standards and procedures of the organization by the employees and to develop a sense of tolerance and respect of human dignity so as to provide safe and secure work environment and promote harmony in the organization.

Need of Discipline:

Discipline is essential for all organizations because:-

- To increase the productivity this is the ultimate goal of any organization.
- To improve the morale of the employee.
- To provide safe and secure work environment for the employees
- To promote harmony in the organization
- To ensure effective coordination between different departments of the organization.
- To promote healthy relationship between and among the employees and management with a view to achieve company's objectives.
- It is moral responsibility of the employer not to allow the minority of employees who are undisciplined to affect the life of majority.

How does Indiscipline arise?

In most of the cases, indiscipline of a worker is the expression of his reaction to his environment. Usually the causes of indiscipline are:

a. Lack of awareness of Company's rules and regulations;
b. False promises made by superiors;
c. Absence of any procedure to handle grievances;
d. No action taken when required;
e. Personal frustrations and misunderstandings.
f. Absence of effective leadership
g. Unfair management practices
h. Communication barriers
a. Non uniform disciplinary action
j. Divide and rule policy adopted by the management instead of trying to treat each employee fairly and equally the management follow divide and then rule policy
k. Inadequate attention to personal problems
ax. Victimization and excessive pressure of the work on subordinate may also lead to indiscipline.

There could be many other different reasons for indiscipline depending upon individual differences.

Concept of discipline:

Positive Discipline: These days the definition of discipline is getting new dimensions as today employees are complying with rules not out of fear of punishment but out of an inherent or inner desire to cooperate and achieve goals. It is possible where the organizational climate is marked by two way communication, clear goals, effective leadership, adequate compensation etc helps employee to be disciplined automatically.

Negative Discipline: Discipline as understood by some of the employees is a sort of check or restrain on their freedom they do not believe in and support discipline, as such they do not follow the rules, regulations and desired standard operating procedure prepared and followed in organization. Thus the disciplinary program forces and contains the employee to obey orders, follow rules and regulations etc through warnings, penalties and other forms f punishment. This approach of discipline is called corrective discipline or negative or punitive discipline. In short negative discipline approach is one in which management puts pressure or hold out threat by imposing penalties on wrongdoers. thus .If employee fails to follow the rules are punished the fear of punishment puts employee back on rails. As defined by Sprigel, Discipline is the force that prompts an individual or a group to observe the rules. —Discipline is the force that prompts an individual or a group to observe the rules, regulations and procedure which are deemed to be necessary to the attainment of the objectivel.

Self Discipline & Control: As Behavioral Scientist believes that discipline is a self control on oneself to achieve organizational objectives According to Megginson self discipline means the training that corrects moulds and strengthens .It refers to one's efforts at self control for the purpose of adjusting oneself to certain needs and demands. This form of discipline is based on two psychological principles which are - first punishment does not always give us desired results and second a self respecting person tends to be better worker than one who is not.

Progressive Discipline: The concept of progressive discipline states that punishment or penalties should be appropriate to the nature of violation. As if inappropriate behavior is of minor type and is never repeated than in that case instead of giving the punishment he should be given an oral warning which will be sufficient in this case. But if violation requires written warning, it must be done according to procedure. After written warning, if the employee still does not follow, than serious punitive action could be taken .In case of major violation employee termination can be the punishment taken.

Misconduct:

Misconduct in general means improper conduct or wrongful behavior. But in case, if we are dealing with employees in an organization, the term misconduct is to be seen with reference to the violations of rules and regulations applicable to the various categories of employees working in the organization.

The following are the common reasons for misconduct:-:

- If the employee does not discharge his duties properly.
- He remain absent from the workplace without any information and leave
- He is found involved in acts which are unsafe for the employer
- If he is grossly immoral and dishonest
- He is insulting, abusive and disturbs the peace of others
- He is unfaithful, corrupt, and disloyal
- He is involved in theft, fraud bribery
- If he does not obey orders and is involved in illegal strikes

- If he cause willful damage to property

Report of Misconduct:

Reporting a complaint is the initiating or starting point of any disciplinary action. For taking disciplinary action against any employee for committed any act of misconduct, the management should specifically get a written complaint. Complaint is nothing but a clear, sequential narration of the facts of incidence of indiscipline by the complainant, in the form of a report to his superior

There are no rigid and specific procedure for taking disciplinary action, the disciplinary procedure followed in Indian Industries usually consists of following steps:

Preliminary Enquiry:

As soon as a complaint is received, the disciplinary authority should conduct a preliminary enquiry which is done with a view to check whether there is enough charges and evidences to proceeded further. If yes in above case than a charge sheet is prepared and issued, preliminary enquiry ends with the issue of charge sheet.

Procedure for Disciplinary Process:

1. **Issuing a letter of charge or charge sheet:** Once it becomes clear after preliminary enquiry that an employee has committed any misconduct, against which disciplinary action is to taken, the letter of charges or

charge sheet is issued against him, which should clearly specify and explain the reason for issuing the charge sheet with all charges should be clearly mentioned, further the charge sheet should ask for an explanation from the employee, the time for answering should be given to the employee.

Charge Sheet: On the basis of preliminary enquiry or otherwise, if the disciplinary authority decides to take disciplinary action against the employee concerned, the first thing to be done is to issue a charge-sheet to delinquent employee.

Charge-sheet is a memorandum of charges or allegations leveled against the employee which are acts of misconduct as per the Conduct, Discipline and Appeal Rules. The Charge-Sheet prepared should be specific and must spell out all the relevant details of the misconduct and should be issued under the signature of Disciplinary Authorities empowered to impose major penalty.

Check-List for preparation of Charge-Sheet: While framing a Charge-sheet, the following items may be kept in mind so that nothing relevant would be missing from the Charge -sheet:

a. Date of charge sheet.
b. Correct Name and Card No. /Employee No. of delinquent employee.
c. Specify date of incident.
d. Description of incident.
e. Reproduce the language in verbatim if there are words of abuse, defamation or threat.
f. Give reference of relevant rules as Conduct, Discipline and Appeal Rules.

g. Specify within how much time and to whom the reply should be submitted.

h. Check the authority competent to issue the Charge-Sheet (See Conduct, Discipline and Appeal Rules or Delegation of Powers, as the case may be).

a. Decide whether employee is to be kept under suspension or not.

j. Decide whom to send the copies of Charge-sheet.

Time for reply to Charge-sheet: A time period should be given to the employee to submit his reply against the Charge-Sheet. Time as stipulated in the Conduct, Discipline & Appeal Rules, but it should not be less than 48 hours from the receipt of the Charge-sheet by the employee and even extensions of time should be given on his request.

Handing over of Charge-sheet: Serving or handing over the Charge-sheet to the delinquent employee is very important in disciplinary proceedings. Therefore, all efforts should be made by the employer to see that the Charge-sheet is served or given on to the delinquent employee.

The Charge-Sheet is handed over to the employee and his signature or thumb-impression is taken on the office copy as an acknowledgement of receiving the charge sheet. In case if he refuses to accept the Charge-sheet, an endorsement to the effect should be made on the office copy in the presence of at least two witnesses whose signatures should be obtained. It can further be displayed on the notice board or if all efforts to serve fail than the copy of charge sheet should be published in local/regional newspaper

2. **Consideration of Explanation**: After getting answer from the employee against the charge sheet, the explanation given by employee should be considered

and if the management is satisfied with the explanation on disciplinary action should be taken, but if not satisfied then there is need for serving a show cause notice

3. **Show Cause Notice:** Show cause notice is issued by the manager when he believes that there is sufficient prima facia evidence of employee misconduct. This however gives employee another chance to heard, once again to reply for misconduct and clear the charges against him. Enquiry should also be initiated by first serving him a notice of enquiry indicating clearly the name of enquiry officer, time, date and place of enquiry

4. **Holding of a full fledge enquiry:** This should be similar as to the procedure of court of law, here also the employee is given equal chance to speak and clear himself and he should be properly heard. When the process of enquiry is over and the findings of the same are recorded, the enquiry officer should suggest the nature of disciplinary action to be taken.

5. **Making a Final Order of Punishment:** At the time of disciplinary action to be taken against employee, when his misconduct is proved his previous records, precedents, effect of action on other employee should also be considered. When the employee feels that the enquiry conducted was not proper and the action taken is unjustified he must be given a chance to make an appeal. He can further appeal to labor court or industrial tribunal.

6. **Follow Up:** After taking the disciplinary action a proper follow up action should be taken and the consequences of the implementation of disciplinary action should be noted and taken care of.

Principles of Natural Justice:

The procedure for taking disciplinary action against any delinquent employee must be based on principles of —natural justice‖ - which state that no man should be held guilty without getting an opportunity to explain his point of view that means he should be given a fair chance:

- to present evidence of his choice
- to cross examine managements evidence
- To explain his point of view without pressure or fear.

Thus to hold an enquiry in conformity with the principles of natural justice, the following conditions are to be met:

      a. the employee should be clearly informed about all the charges levelled against him;
      b. the witnesses should be examined ordinarily in the presence of the employee in relation with the Charges;
      c. the employee should be given a fair opportunity to cross-examine the witnesses;
      d. the employee should be given a fair opportunity to examine his own witnesses, including himself in his defence, if he so

wishes;

   e. the enquiry officer records his findings with reasons for the same in his report

Punishment:

Depending on the gravity of misconduct, management may initiate various types of punishment/penalties. These punishment or penalties can be divided into major penalties and minor penalties.

Minor penalties: it include

- Oral Warning
- Written Reprimand
- Loss of privileges
- Fines
- Suspension

Major penalties it include

- Withholding increment,
- Demotions or stopping transfer
- Discharge
- Dismissal

Essentials of a Good Disciplinary System:

The essentials of good disciplinary system are:

- **Knowledge of rules**: The management and the employees must be clearly informed and aware of right code of conduct to be followed in the organisation.

- **Prompt Action**: All violations of rules and regulations and misconduct should be promptly enquired and taken decision this will make employee aware of punishment this will scare him to violate in future.

- **Fair Action**: All acts of indiscipline should be punished uniformly and constituently, ie all employees should receive same punishment for the same offense.

- **Well define Procedure**: The procedure to be used for disciplinary action should be clear, precise and properly lay down and should be informed to all.

- **Constructive approach**: the management should ensure that disciplinary should be preventative than punitive in nature. Focus should be preventing employees to violate the rules rather than on giving punishment after violation of rules.

  - **Review & Revision**: All rules and regulations should be periodically reviewed to check that they are as according to the changing time and should also be revised as according to the time.

COUNSELING:

Emotions are part of the nature of human beings and emotional upsets are part of their life. It is sometimes more disastrous to suppress emotions. The emotional problems affect the interest of the employees and the organization in which he is working for. The problems may reduce their productivity, morale and increase absenteeism. Hence the managers should take steps to maintain a reasonable emotional balance of their employees and channelize their emotions on the constructive lines. The instrument with which the managers can achieve such balance is called ***Counseling.***

Counseling is a method of understanding and helping people who have technical, personal and emotional or adjustment problems that usually has emotional contents that an employee with the objective of reducing it so that performance is maintained at adequate level or even improved upon Counseling.

According to Ghosh and Ghorpade —Personal counseling is defined as discussion of an emotional problem with an employee, with the general objective of reducing it so that performance is maintained at adequate level or even improved upon.‖

As defined by Keith Davis counseling involves discussion of problem that usually has emotional content with an employee in order to help the employee to improve his emotional and mental state.

Counseling involves a relationship between the counselor (manager) and the counselee (employee) characterized by trust and openness where counselor tries to help counselee to come out of his emotional and mental state of depression.

The main purpose of Counseling is to help an emotionally disturbed employee to become normal, develop self confidence, self control, and understanding so that he can work effectively.

Features of Counseling:

1. Counseling involves interviewing the person being counseled and helping to solve his problems through human approach of sharing and guidance.

2. Counseling involves sitting down in private setting for an open discussion with an employee. It maybe for

- Sometimes to pay a sincere compliment to the employee
- Sometimes to solve a problem that is hurting productivity/effectiveness
- Sometimes it is because an employee violated your discipline line

and you need to talk about improvement in his behavior.

3. Counseling is a two way dialogue and not one way sermonizing or advising.

4. It encourages the other person to to talk about himself so that the problem and the right reason for the problem due to which problem emerged can be clearly identified and on that basis solutions can be worked out.

5. In an organization, counseling can be done by the team leader, supervisor or manager or one can seek the expertise and assistance of an in-house or external professional counselor.

Causes/ Needs of Counseling:

Some of the conditions like frustration, lack of job satisfaction, resistance to change, intergroup of conflict, interpersonal relationship etc are the major causes of counseling needs. Given below is a causes for which Counseling is required. list of common situations that require urgent need for counseling from a superior to his subordinate:

- Conflict: conflict arises when there is disagreement between two or more individuals or groups and each employee or group tries to gain acceptance of its view or objective over the other. Conflict is undesirable in any sector and therefore should be avoided and resolved as soon as possible.
- Stress: stress is a condition of strain that has a direct bearing or emotions through processes and physical condition of a person.
- Stress are of two types
- On the job stress; the job itself may be basic cause of stress. Employees may not be able to cope with the demands of the job due to which employee feel pressure work overload, tension anxiety etc.
- Off the job stress: the reason for this types of stress is numerous which include financial problems, death in the family, martial problem, problem with children.
- When an employee violates the standards of the organisation.
- When an employee is consistently late or absent.
- When an employee's productivity starts to go down.
- When one employee behaves in such a way that productivity of others is negatively affected.
- When two employees have a conflict that is becoming public and it is affecting the work.
- When you want to compliment an individual.
- When you want to delegate a new task.

Types of Counseling:

There are three types of Counseling:

- **Directive Counseling:** It is the process of hearing person's emotional problems, deciding what he should do and then encouraging and motivating him to do. Under this type of Counseling the counselor performs all the functions of Counseling except reorientation.

- **Non directive Counseling:** It is also called as client centered Counseling as it is the process of skillfully listening to a person encouraging him to explain his emotional problems, understand them and determine the course of action. Its main focus is on the counselee that is why it is called client centered Counseling, professional counselors generally follow non directive Counseling. They help the counselee in discovering and finding a suitable course of action by himself. This is very effective type of Counseling but it has some disadvantages also like it is time consuming, it requires professional counselors, it is costly etc.

- **Participative counseling:** As per Indian organizational situation, participative Counseling appears to be more practical and suitable as it is in the middle of directive and non directive Counseling. It involves mental relationship between counselor and counselee that establish a cooperative exchange of ideas, information, knowledge, values feelings etc to solve the problem of counselee. It is not dominated by either of the party.

Functions of Counseling:

There are many functions of Counseling which are:

- **Advice**: In Counseling, the counselor after carefully listening to the problems counselee, make judgment about his problems and guide him towards desired course of actions.

- **Reassurance**: Reassurance provides courage, confidence and strength and develops a positive feeling to the employee ensuring him that he has chosen the right course of action and is on the right track.

- **Clarified thinking**: It is the important function of Counseling as it encourages person to think in rationale and realistic manner. It helps employee to take responsibility

- **Release of Emotional Tension**: It is another important function of Counseling, as when person share his emotional problem with someone they free themselves from their tension and frustration. This emotional release may not solve the problem but paves way of solution.

- **Communication**: It helps employee to communicate and release his tension and get free of stress.

- **Reorientation**: Counseling help people in recognizing and accepting their strengths, weakness and limitations.

Counseling Process:

The Counseling process normally consists of the following stages:

Initiating: This involves developing mutual understanding openness and acceptance between counselors and counseled. This rapport building is essential to initiate the Counseling.

Exploration: This involved understanding with the help of the Counseling, the counselee's own situation, his feelings, his strengths and weakness, his problems and needs.

The counselor allows the counselee to talk about anything even apparently unrelated to the issue. It is important for the counselor to achieve a free flow of expression-often through rumblings – of the employee. The counselor will need an alert and receptive mind for this. The counselor, however, see to it that the counselor eventually concentrates his thoughts on his problem rather than stray away from it. The counselor has to help the counselee in concentrating more on the problem and getting deeper into it and to discover the basic problems by himself.

Formulation of action plan: This involved exploring possible solutions and formulating action plan for implementing them to make the counselee the normal person.

SUMMARY:

Job satisfaction is the combination of psychological, physiological and environmental circumstances that causes person to truthfully say —I am satisfied with my job‖. Satisfaction involves positive emotional state. It is an end feeling which influence the subsequent behavior. It is an employee general attitude towards his job.

In this unit we have also studied about organizational culture which means values, beliefs, attitudes and behavioral patterns shared by organizational members in relation to organizational goals, which gives the organization a unique character. Research findings have suggested that organizational culture seems to be a sophisticated approach to understand the beliefs and attitudes of individual members about their respective organizations (Brown, 1998). Now days organizational culture is been given huge importance as compared to factors such as structure, strategy or politics because of the fact that organizational culture was perceived to be offering a non-mechanistic, flexible and imaginative approach to understanding how organizations work (Brown, 1998). Consequently, organizational culture is considered to be the great —cure-all‖ for most organizational problems (Wilson, 1992).

Discipline is required for both the organization and individual. In the organisationit is needed to regulate the behavior of people, maintain peace and channel their efforts towards organizational goals. Sad to state, most people do not exercise self discipline and this fact makes external control necessary for bringing order within an organization.

In the present fast moving society, the employee has to face numerous problems which may be personal in nature or may be related to the job. In such situation counseling helps in reducing the stressful conditions, Counseling tries to improve the mental health of the employee so that employee not only become physically fit but also mentally alert, ie the emotions are channelized on constructive lines so that employees develop self confidence, self control and work effectively

KEY TERMS:

Change Management : The deliberate effort of an organization to anticipate change and to manage its introduction, implementation, and consequences.

Counseling: It is a method of understanding and helping people who have technical, personal and emotional or adjustment problems and guiding them on the correct path.

Cultural Change: A change in a company's shared values and aims.

Discipline: A procedure that corrects or punishes a subordinate because a rule, instructions of organization has been violated. It is basically the code of conduct of the organization to be followed by the employee.

Disciplinary procedure: procedure carried out in the workplace in the event of an employee committing some act contrary to terms of the employment agreement. If the act is regarded as Gross Misconduct this may lead to Summary Dismissal.

Domestic Enquiry: A chance given to an accused person to defend himself by bringing his own witness and other evidence.

Dismissal: termination from employment due to any misconduct

Hierarchy of needs: A psychology theory ascribed to Abraham H. Maslow in which he proposed that people will constantly seek to have their basic needs (sleep, food, water, shelter, etc.) fulfilled and that such needs ultimately determine behavior.

Job satisfaction: it implies appositive emotional state. Its employee's positive attitude towards his job.

Misconduct: Violation of established rules and norms of behavior.

Organizational culture: It is a system of shared assumptions, values, and beliefs, which controls how people behave in the organizations. These are standard guidelines which are decided by the management which make the organization separate from one another.

Organizational Development (OD): A method aimed at changing attitude, values, and beliefs of employees so that employees can improve the organization culture.

Standing order: service rules and other agreed terms of employment certified by an authority as per the provision of the Industrial Employment

The Author

Dr. Anshumali Pandey, is a renowned & reliable name in the field of Education, Hospitality, Tourism and Tribal Food. He is a Teacher and Chef by profession, and also an Author, a Business Auditor, and an avid culinary traveller to the Indian Sub continental hinterlands. Dr. Anshumali Pandey is a Hospitality Educator (PhD) who specialises in Higher Education, Office Administration, Pay roll, HR, Labour Laws, Audit, and Procurement & Tender Process. He is an Author with 47 Publications consisting of 32 Books.

The books written by Dr Anshumali Pandey are essentially a banquet arising from an experience of over 25 years of Professional life and have boiled down to crisp and accurate writing on his favourite subjects. Hospitality Sector champion requires to be a specialist in many fields and Dr Pandey is one of them. His knowledge is evident from the spectrum of subjects which he has chosen for his books so far, which ranges from being a specialist chef, to Master of Human resources, to Education and to love for children, and topped with Spirituality.

Books written by the Author are –

1. Theory of Indian Cookery
2. Beauty and Irony of Silvassa Tourism
3. A Short Indian Food Story
4. Be Your Own Guide to Indian Cuisine
5. Cookery Fundamentals
6. History of Indian Food
7. The Great Indian Story Book for Children
8. Personal Budget: Easy Work Book
9. Online Classes Log Book

10. Dictionary Making Work Book for School Children
11. The Lazy Bed
12. Hindu Dharm (हिन्दू धर्म) (In Hindi Language)
13. Where is my coffee?
14. Your First Job is Never your Last (Volume 1)
15. You are Almost There (Quick Fix Resume and Interview Hacks)
16. Working for the Enemy? - A lesson in Career Management
17. Public Speaking for the Young
18. A Date With Coffee
19. How to be The Best Hotel Front Office Employee
20. Diploma in Food Production, The complete Syllabus
21. Diploma in F&B Service, The Complete Syllabus
22. Diploma in Front Office, The Complete Syllabus
23. The Time to Speak is Now
24. Munshi Premchand (Short Stories in English)
25. The Housekeeping Department, Text Book
26. Hitchhiker's Guide to Trekking in Uttarakhand
27. Uttarakhand, A divine Land for a Reason
28. Bachhon ke liye rochak kahaniyan (बच्चों के लिए रोचक कहानियाँ) (In Hindi Language)
29. Basic Communication Skills of English
30. The Basic Office Organisation Book for Start-ups
31. Hospitality HRM
32. Hospitality Marketing

Connect with me: anshumali.pandey@gmail.com
https://notionpress.com/author/337004

Dr Anshumali Pandey, PhD, Author.

Scan the QR code to check latest updates of the Author's works.

www.ingramcontent.com/pod-product-compliance
Lightning Source LLC
Chambersburg PA
CBHW021524150726
47990CB00006B/2086